Oracle Shell Scripting
Linux and UNIX Programming for Oracle

Jon Emmons

This book is dedicated to all those who have inspired, supported, and believed in me:

> *My parents Rachael and Bruce*
> *My sister Carla*
> *Kirsten Mohring*
> *Bob Bean*

Thank you all.

Oracle Shell Scripting
Linux and UNIX Programming for Oracle

By Jon Emmons

Copyright © 2007 by Rampant TechPress. All rights reserved.

Printed in the United States of America.

Published by Rampant TechPress, Kittrell, North Carolina, USA

Oracle In-Focus Series: Book #26

Series Editor: Don Burleson

Editors: Teri Wade

Production Editor: Teri Wade

Cover Design: Janet Burleson

Printing History: August, 2007 for First Edition

ISBN-10: 0977671550
ISBN-13: 978-0977671557
Library of Congress Control Number: 2007933681

Table of Contents

Conventions Used in this Book

It is critical for any technical publication to follow rigorous standards and employ consistent punctuation conventions to make the text easy to read.

However, this is not an easy task. Within Oracle there are many types of notation that can confuse a reader. Some Oracle utilities such as STATSPACK and TKPROF are always spelled in CAPITAL letters, while Oracle parameters and procedures have varying naming conventions in the Oracle documentation. It is also important to remember that many Oracle commands are case sensitive, and are always left in their original executable form, and never altered with italics or capitalization.

Hence, all Rampant TechPress books follow these conventions:

- Parameters - All Oracle parameters will be lowercase italics. Exceptions to this rule are parameter arguments that are commonly capitalized (KEEP pool, TKPROF), these will be left in ALL CAPS.

- Variables – All PL/SQL program variables and arguments will also remain in lowercase italics (*dbms_job, dbms_utility*).

- Tables & dictionary objects – All data dictionary objects are referenced in lowercase italics (*dba_indexes, v$sql*). This includes all v$ and x$ views (*x$kcbcbh, v$parameter*) and dictionary views (*dba_tables, user_indexes*).

- SQL – All SQL is formatted for easy use in the code depot, and all SQL is displayed in lowercase. The main SQL terms (select, from, where, group by, order by, having) will always appear on a separate line.

- Programs & Products – All products and programs that are known to the author are capitalized according to the vendor specifications (IBM, DBXray, etc). All names known by Rampant TechPress to be trademark names appear in this text as initial caps. References to UNIX are always made in uppercase.

Preface

It is essential to today's Oracle professional to streamline and, whenever possible, automate repetitive tasks. With duties ranging from system set up and maintenance to interfacing with functional users to capacity planning the less time you have to spend on monotonous tasks like reviewing logs and checking for free space the more productive you can be.

There are several commercial solutions available for automating tasks, but many of the best tools for performing complex tasks, monitoring services and automating common administration duties are already included on your UNIX and Linux systems. Most of these tools, like the Bash shell, have been around for decades with few changes to their basic functionality.

In this book we will examine how to customize your environment and then look at the important aspects of shell scripting including some of the most commonly used tools. Finally we will look at several pre-made scripts for everything from checking for errors in a database alert log to monitoring the load on a system.

Those already familiar with shell scripting will find this book a handy reference. Syntax is included for the common options for many commands and the included scripts can be used as is or used as a starting point for custom scripts.

Throughout this book an emphasis has been placed on simplicity. Far too often a script is adapted to perform several disparate tasks making it difficult to maintain and even more difficult for new people to learn. In some cases similar tasks should be combined, but when the type of tasks, frequency of tasks or user base differ it is often better to create separate scripts. You will see this reflected in the scripts in the final section of this book.

Like any technical skill the more you work with shell scripts the better you will get at it. While this book is just a starting point it will give you a firm foundation in the fundamentals of shell scripting and a good collection of scripts to implement or modify for your own purposes. You will also gain the skills needed to modify and troubleshoot scripts written by others.

UNIX and Shell Scripting

Common Ground

The aim of this first chapter is to make sure we are all starting with a common understanding of the UNIX environment. If you have been using UNIX for a while some of this chapter will be review, but the information here will make things easier as we get into shell scripting.

Getting started with UNIX can be quite intimidating. Many experienced Oracle professionals are completely overwhelmed by the command prompt and who can blame them? In a graphical user interface (GUI) like Microsoft Windows you have somewhere to go, something to click on, a checkbox or a menu. At the UNIX command prompt it is just you and a blinking cursor.

Don't panic! Nothing is ever hard in UNIX; it is just that things are often far less than obvious. Throughout this book you will be exposed to the tools and tricks that will help you manage your Oracle instances and the skills that will help you get around with ease. First we will cover a little about how we got to this point.

```
$
```

Figure 1.1: *This may be all you see when logging into a UNIX machine*

This first chapter is just a little background on UNIX and Linux. Some of this information may seem trivial, but it is important to

---

have a little background information when we are referring to an operating system with roots that go back to the 1960s.

UNIX and its many flavors

UNIX is a group of computer operating systems. Just like Microsoft Windows it controls the computer hardware, does it's best to keep all your devices playing nicely together and gives you an interface to run things on the computer. Unlike Microsoft Windows there are several companies who make UNIX operating systems but they must all comply with the Single UNIX Specification and be certified as such in order to be called UNIX. Some popular versions of UNIX are Solaris, AIX, HP-UX and Tru64.

Many more operating systems are UNIX-like. These systems meet many, or possibly even all of the characteristics specified in the Single UNIX Specification, however have not been certified. Of these UNIX-like operating systems Linux is by far the most prominent. Conversationally Linux is often referred to as UNIX, though it is not currently certified as such.

The information about UNIX in this book can all be applied to Linux except where specifically noted.

Why UNIX?

Why in an age with 512MB video cards would you ever choose an operating system where your primary interface is a text-only command line? Well, there are plenty of advantages, but stability is a big one. UNIX has been around since the 1960s and, though the developers at that time could not have anticipated the needs of the early 21st century, UNIX is a perfect fit for our modern multi-user multi-tasking environment.

The UNIX standard also provides a vendor-neutral set of tools and interfaces which programmers can use when developing software. This allows developers to adapt their software to different versions of UNIX more easily than between non-UNIX systems.

UNIX and UNIX-like operating systems like to be in charge. Even a small UNIX system is capable of handling hundreds of users running thousands of tasks simultaneously. With a very strict permissions structure and strong controls on how and when things happen on the system, UNIX offers a very stable and secure environment ideal for running Oracle.

What is a shell?

A shell in UNIX is the software which allows you, a human, interact with the inner workings of the UNIX operating system. Because of the shell we get to use commands that resemble our natural language, though sometimes only just barely, to control the behavior of the computer. There are other types of shells in computing, but this is the only type we will be concerned with for this book.

Beyond the ability to use somewhat intuitive commands individually, the shell also gives us the ability to combine these commands into shell scripts. A shell script can contain one command or hundreds and the commands could be nearly anything you could do from within the shell. Shell scripts may be used for something as simple as displaying a message or something as complicated as shutting down an Oracle database, backing up all files associated with it, then starting it back up.

You can access a UNIX shell in many different ways. You may access the shell by sitting at a UNIX or UNIX-like computer where the shell is displayed on screen or you may use a secure protocol to enter a shell on a system thousands of miles away.

sh, bash and other shells

There are, of course, many kinds of shells. Each has its strengths and weaknesses but my preference is to use the Bourne (sh) shell for shell scripting and the Bourne-Again Shell (bash) as my default shell when logging in to a system.

The Bourne shell was released in 1977 by AT&T Bell Laboratories and is currently included on all UNIX and most UNIX-like operating systems. As shells go the Bourne shell is fairly straight-forward in its syntax. This, combined with its ubiquity and the fact that many other shells are based on it make it a great shell to learn.

What the Bourne shell offers in stability it lacks in modern features and the everyday user of the Bourne shell would miss out on some usability improvements. Thankfully the Bourne Again Shell (commonly referred to as bash) came along ten years later with many upgrades from the Bourne shell. Some of the biggest time saving features are a command history which can be recalled by pressing the up-arrow and the ability to complete partially typed file names by pressing the tab key.

Experienced programmers often prefer to write shell scripts in shells which more closely resemble the programming languages they are familiar with (the C shell for instance.) Other shells such as the Korn and Z shells include features from the Bourne and C shells and even more advanced features for shell scripting such as associative arrays.

While the tasks we are concerned about in this book could be accomplished in any shell it is the omnipresence of the Bourne shell which makes it my favorite. Additionally since it is the foundation of many of the other popular shells much of the syntax found in this book will work in other shells. These properties make Bourne shell scripts very portable.

On occasion I may show a script in another shell such as Korn. If I do I will make a specific point to mention why that shell is used and the syntax differences.

The Bourne Again Shell is also common, though not quite as common as Bourne, and the additional features provide an improved user experience. Believe me, once you are used to tab-completion and hitting the up arrow to recall a recent command you won't be able to live without them.

If you do have a compelling reason to use a shell other than Bourne and bash go ahead. Most shells are well documented and, as mentioned above the Bourne syntax will work in many other shells as well. I strongly suggest whatever shell you choose, choose a shell and stick with it. The small differences between shells often end up causing the most frustration.

Every time you open a command line session you will start in your default shell. On most systems you can just type the command echo $SHELL and the shell you're using will be printed on the screen. The default shell is initially assigned when an account is created but it can be easily changed after the point. The default shell will be covered a bit more in chapter 4.

If you find you need to switch shells temporarily you can do so by typing the full path to the desired shell. This can be very useful for troubleshooting and is fully explained in chapter 3.

The UNIX kernel

The heart of a UNIX system is its kernel. The kernel interacts with the computer's hardware and makes certain resources such as memory, disk and processor available to other software running on the system.

The kernel also controls communication between different applications. By controlling not only what applications can do, but what they can do to each other, the kernel maintains total control over the system. It is this control that gives UNIX its outstanding security and stability. No user or process can bypass the control of the kernel.

Memory and swap

As mentioned above, the memory (RAM) in a UNIX system is controlled by the kernel. Through requests to the kernel an application can obtain space in memory. This happens every time an application is started. When an application closes, the kernel reclaims the memory and that space can be given out again.

UNIX systems also employ disk for use as virtual memory. This virtual memory is called swap. Since disk is considerably cheaper than RAM, space is partitioned off to use as an overflow in case we run out of physical RAM.

The way a UNIX system uses swap is a bit more complicated than explained here. Just keep in mind that if you use all your real memory the machine will have to start heavily using the much slower swap space. This can slow the machine down to a crawl causing performance problems and in some cases making things fail altogether.

Processes

When an application is run on a UNIX system it is created as a process. While the kernel has control over all the processes on the system, individual processes can start child processes to perform additional work.

At any given time a UNIX machine is running several processes. Some of these are just what the system needs to operate; others belong to users on the system. While there can be hundreds or more processes running on a system at once only one process can actually be executing on a processor at a time. The system will give the appearance of running many things at once by quickly switching between different processes.

UNIX allows you to view what processes are running. While this is a tremendous help when troubleshooting since other users may be able to see what commands you are executing you must be careful not to reveal passwords when you execute a command. Chapter 10 will cover more about these issues.

Files and file systems

UNIX and Linux use a hierarchical file system. This means that just like Microsoft Windows, there are folders (more often referred to as directories in UNIX) which can contain files or other folders.

Individual drives are often split into separate logical drives called partitions. Instead of having all the partitions in one place on a system, UNIX will allow them to be mounted practically anywhere. This, and the ability to mount disks from another system on the network makes storage very flexible as you can add a drive anywhere you need it.

If you are familiar with Microsoft Windows the first difference you will notice is that a forward slash (/) is used in UNIX where a backslash (\) would be used in Windows. This just takes a little time to retrain your fingers. A little tougher to understand may be that there is no My Computer that contains all your drives.

All file systems in UNIX begin at the root directory. This is often referred to as slash. All other directories in UNIX are a subdirectory of slash. In slash there are several key directories. Here are a few of them:

DIRECTORY	DESCRIPTION
/	the slash partition is where everything starts
/bin	contains many commands that will be used as executable binaries
/lib	software libraries required for binaries in /bin
/usr/local	reserved for installed software 'local' to this computer
/etc	system-wide configuration files for this computer
/tmp or /var/tmp	temporary files for this system or any applications on it
/u01 – /u99	directories conventionally used for Oracle software and data (when using Optimal Flexible Architecture or OFA)

Table 1.1: *Some Important UNIX directories*

In addition to these important directories each user is assigned a home directory. A user's home directory will be where the user is taken when he logs into a system and is typically different for each user. Home directories are often in the path /home/*username* but this is far less than standard. The home directory offers a useful place to keep your files separate from other users.

Why Shell Scripting?

Shell scripting is all about saving you time. Here are a few ways it is likely to help save time:

▪ Combine multiple commands into a single shell script

- Take commands you regularly have to execute and schedule them to run automatically

- Save time looking up commands by placing them in shell scripts

- Instead of teaching complex commands to others, script them

- Regularly monitor logs and the environment to identify and rectify problems before they cause downtime

Let's look at an example. Here is what you might have to do to make an export of the database 'mydb'.

```
$ ORACLE_SID=mydb
$ export $ORACLE_SID
$ exp USERID=system/manager FULL=y BUFFER=8388608 \
> FILE=/u01/backup/exports/mydb/mydb.exp
```

Maybe you can remember all that, but I can not; especially that big buffer number that represents 8MB but must be specified in bytes. There is also a high probability of typos in big commands like this and forgetting something like setting the ORACLE_SID variable, which is what the first and second line do, can result in exporting the wrong database altogether.

Code Depot Username = reader, Password = shell

The good news is now that we have figured out all the commands we need it is trivial to write a shell script to do all this. The details will be explored a little later, but here is what the finished script would look like:

```
#!/bin/sh
ORACLE_SID=mydb
export $ORACLE_SID
exp USERID=system/manager FULL=y BUFFER=8388608 \
FILE=/u01/backup/exports/mydb/mydb.exp
echo "Database exported to /u01/backup/exports/mydb/mydb.exp"
echo "Grab it there and send them to the boss."
```

Looks familiar right? The first line is a special hint to tell the operating system what to use to run this shell script, but more about that later. The rest of the script is exactly what was typed to run these commands manually! Simple shell scripts can be just this easy.

Now to export whenever your boss tells you he needs it. You are on vacation this week, but the boss needs the export. If you are doing them manually there is a chance you are going to get a call at home asking you to "run that thing you do for the boss when he asks for it." That is no good.

Instead you take the extra few minutes to make a shell script out of it. The Friday before your vacation you mention to a coworker "If the boss asks for the export of mydb, just log on and run *mydb_export.sh* and give him the file it creates." Now, without your coworker, who might not even be a DBA, having the burden of trying to remember the exp command and parameters, the export can go off seamlessly. The echo commands at the end of the script even provide some useful output to help your coworker get everything right. You can continue to enjoy your vacation and everyone gets what they need.

The shell, Oracle and you

It is important to know at this point that you have probably been using a UNIX shell already. Any time you connect to a command line interface on a UNIX machine, whether via a terminal window on the host machine or a networked connection like telnet, rsh, ssh or serial you are using some type of shell. This is what is referred to as the interactive mode of the shell.

In interactive mode the shell interprets what you type and causes certain things to happen on the machine. For instance, you have probably opened a shell and typed the command sqlplus to start a SQL session. After you hit enter the shell first checks to see if sqlplus is a keyword then goes about finding something named sqlplus in one of the locations you have specified in your $PATH variable. Do not worry if you have not specified your $PATH variable. It is probably already set up, though not necessarily optimally. That will be covered more in chapter 4.

If the shell finds something called sqlplus in one of the locations from your $PATH variable it will try to run it. If that sqlplus is an executable application you should then see the application start. At this point it will appear that you have left the UNIX shell, but this is not exactly the case. The program sqlplus is actually running as a child process of the shell. It is conventional, though not completely accurate, to say that sqlplus is running in the shell. This is reinforced when we type exit to leave sqlplus and are returned to the shell prompt right where we left off.

This interactive use of the UNIX shell is something with which most Oracle professionals are familiar and comfortable. For the bulk of this book we are going to focus on using the shell in non-interactive mode (often referred to as batch mode.) In non-interactive mode commands are read from a file rather than a keyboard but the steps for processing them are the same. Files are read one line at a time and interpreted by the shell. Decisions, such as if and while statements, are often used in this mode, though they can be used in interactive mode as well.

When we execute a shell script it will run in non-interactive mode. Since both interactive and non-interactive modes of a shell behave very similarly it is often useful for troubleshooting to run commands from a shell script one by one in interactive mode. There are a few differences between these modes which can make troubleshooting difficult. These differences will be covered in chapter 3.

When to script

A shell script can be written to do anything that can be done at the command line. So when do you want to write a shell script? When is it a bad idea? Well, here are a few guidelines.

Shell scripts can yield the biggest return on regular tasks that are performed more-or-less the same way each time. If every day you log into a system and remove some files out of a directory, backup a database, or check a log file for a specific string of characters, you should automate these tasks. Chances are you can make them run automatically and save yourself the hassle all together.

Shell scripts are not just for automation though. Take the example of the export script given at the beginning of this chapter. This specific example is not one you would automatically run. As specified, it only needs to be run when the boss asks for this export. In this case the script saves time in a different way by providing the ability to type *mydb_export.sh* instead of trying to remember all the right parameters for the exp command.

One of the most powerful features of the shell and shell scripting is the ability to affect several files and even multiple servers with a single script. Loops and commands such as *find* make shell scripting ideal for managing large numbers of files in a single step.

In general, there is little point in writing a shell script to do something once. The exception to this is the occasion when something needs to be run at a time when you would rather not have to be around. In this case you may decide to bundle those commands into a shell script and schedule it to run without your involvement. Be careful with this type of script and always be thinking "what if something goes wrong?" because sooner or later it will and if you are not around to fix it, you could get in some hot water.

A warning about script bloat

If I have done a good job selling you on the benefits of shell scripting you might be thinking "This is great! I'll just script everything I do!" Be careful. Having a couple hundred shell scripts around might sound like it will save you hours a day but chances are you will get to a point where you can not remember all your shell scripts!

You also need to be sensitive to others who may use the same system you do. What is a shortcut to you may be a distraction to them. The other hazard of scripting is once you have scripted something you may forget how to do it. Sooner or later you will be on a system without your library of shell scripts and you will be wracking your brain to remember how to do something. This is when it is useful to have a copy of your shell scripts handy and I recommend keeping an updated copy of all your scripts on your personal computer for reference.

Building a shell script

Sometimes building a shell script will be easy. If you type the same commands with the same options and always get the same result you can just about put the commands into a file and run it. More often you will have to deal with the possibility that one or more of the commands could fail, that the environment could change, and even that you may need different input on different days.

While later sections of this book will tell you how to handle these in more detail, here are some high level considerations to building shell scripts:

- What are you trying to accomplish
- What are the dependencies
  - Which dependencies can we check first
  - Which dependencies cannot be checked
- How broad will the effects of this script be
- What happens if any step fails
  - Should the script continue or be halted
- What results or output do we want from the script
  - Who should be notified of the results and how
- What cleanup should be done when the script is complete
- What if two copies of the script get executed simultaneously

Perhaps the most important part of planning your script is handling failures. Sooner or later someone will remove a file, fill a disk, or cause some other problem beyond your control and it is important to know your script will not just keep marching on assuming everything is OK.

If you consider all these points before you start writing a script the process will be quick and the result will be a script that does what you want it to.

Conclusion

This chapter gave some background on UNIX and UNIX-like operating systems. This type of system has been around for decades and, though there are several versions of it available today, they all share a common set of tools.

The shell was introduced as the software which allows a person to interact with a UNIX or UNIX-like system. The Bourne and Bourne Again shells were introduced as the shells of choice for shell scripting and interactive use respectively.

Some important UNIX directories were introduced with a little background on what you are likely to find there. Though not guaranteed you will find these directories on most UNIX and Linux systems.

Shell scripting is a great way to combine multiple commands into a single shell script to simplify multi-step tasks. Once combined into a shell script, regular tasks can be scheduled to happen automatically.

You are probably already using the UNIX shell in an interactive mode when you connect to your system. Most of the things you do in an interactive shell will apply when you are writing shell scripts.

Your first shell scripts will likely contain commands you have typed in an interactive shell session. Though there are some differences between interactive and non-interactive mode, these scripts are quick to write and should start saving you time almost immediately.

As you start writing more complex scripts it is important to have a clear idea of the goals of the script, dependencies, and possible problems. Specific consideration should be given to possible points of failure within the script.

The next chapter will explore the building blocks of shell scripting. If you have done some programming, the concepts will be familiar to you. If not, no need to worry, scripting is usually less complicated than other programming. Just take it one step at a time.

Key Concepts

Now is probably a good time to take a step back and make sure we have all the tools we need to get started with shell scripting.

Getting to your shell

Most of the work we are going to do will be done at the command line shell. You are probably familiar with some of the methods for getting to your shell but we will cover them briefly here just to make sure we consider all the options.

The most straight forward way of getting to your shell is via a keyboard and monitor connected directly to the system on which you will be working. Depending on your configuration you may find a text-only login or a full graphical user interface here. While this approach has the obvious benefit of simplicity, excluding variables such as the network and client system, it is often inhospitable to work in noisy server rooms. Also many servers do not even come with a video card, completely excluding this option.

Most UNIX and Linux systems have one or more ways to connect directly to the machine through a serial port typically located on the back of the system. While useful for administration tasks when there is a problem, this method also requires physical access to the machine. This is not how we want to connect to our system on a day-to-day basis.

Telnet and rlogin are two methods which can be used to connect to a system over the network. Both of these options have the advantage of allowing you to connect from a system which is physically in a different location; however, these options do not offer any type of encryption. They may expose what you are typing to others on the same network or any network in between the system you are working on and the server. For this reason telnet and rlogin are no longer the preferred method of connecting to a system.

The secure shell protocol (SSH) is the most popular and recommended way to remotely connect to UNIX and Linux systems. SSH offers a very high level of security by encrypting the commands you type and the output you see.

Most Linux and UNIX systems now come with SSH installed and configured. Unless your network administrator is blocking the SSH protocol for some reason, you should be able to use an SSH client to make a shell connection to the system on which you want to work. There are many commercial and free SSH client programs available for Windows. A good free option is PuTTY by Simon Tatham. This application is small, free and flexible and should work on most Windows versions.

Those who wish to connect from a Linux, UNIX or Mac OSX machine already have an SSH client. All you need to do is locate the Terminal application which will allow you to open a command line shell on the local system. You can then type *ssh username@hostname* to connect to the host you wish to work on. Your username and password should have been given to you by your system administrator.

What shell am I in?

Once you connect to a system, whether directly on the system's keyboard or through a remote connection you will automatically start in your default shell. The default shell was originally assigned to you when your account was created.

To find out what shell you are currently using we can use the *echo* command:

```
$ echo $SHELL
/bin/bash
```

In this command we are using the *echo* command to examine the value of the environment variable *$SHELL*. This variable was set by the system when we started this command line session and shows the full path to the shell we were assigned at login. Here are some common shells you might see:

- /bin/sh – Bourne shell
- /bin/bash – Bourne Again shell
- /bin/csh – C shell
- /bin/ksh – Korn shell
- /bin/tcsh – TC shell
- /bin/zsh – Z shell

Shell binaries are also commonly found in the /usr/local/bin directory. Consult your system administrator if you are having trouble finding your shell binaries.

Switching shells on-the-fly

It can be useful to temporarily change your shell to test shell scripts or commands in a different shell. To temporarily change shells we can execute the desired shell right from the current one like in the following example:

```
$ sh
$ exit
exit
$ ksh
$ exit
```

By typing the command name for the desired shell, you enter that shell from within the current one. To exit the sub-shell, type *exit* to return to the original shell session. In the example given above, we have entered the Bourne shell, exited then entered and exited the Korn shell.

Many of the common shells use the same format for the prompt. Because of this you should not change shells unnecessarily since it can make it very difficult to keep track of what shell you are in. Also the *$SHELL* variable is not updated when you enter another shell making it even more difficult to tell what shell you are in.

The next chapter will look at how to change the default login shell so you will not have to worry about switching so much.

Differences between interactive and non-interactive modes

So far we have been talking about methods to connect to the shell in interactive mode. Interactive mode allows users to enter commands and receive feedback from the shell. As commands are combined into shell scripts, these scripts will be run in a non-interactive mode.

In an interactive mode the shell will look for some special files including /etc/profile and .profile in the user's home directory.

Shell variables and aliases can be set in these files for all users on the system or just for individual users. We will spend some time customizing these in the next chapter.

In non-interactive mode the shell will not look for these files. This is significant because the absence of shell variables and aliases can cause some commands to behave differently in non-interactive mode than they do in interactive mode.

Commands, options, arguments and input

Since we will be covering a lot of information about UNIX commands it is important to clear up some of the terminology that will be used.

There are three distinctly different things which make up what we refer to as a command. There is the command or script name which comes first, options, which typically come second, and arguments which typically come after options. The order for options and arguments may be different or they may even be omitted altogether.

The first part, the command or script name, will sometimes be referred to as the command. For example, we say "the *ls* command. Shell scripts allow us to combine multiple commands into a single script that can then appear to be a command itself. For the most part, it is transparent whether we are calling a binary command, a shell internal command, or a script.

Whether calling a command, internal or script we will frequently use options or arguments to modify the behavior of the script. Options follow the command, typically begin with a dash (-), and can be made up of characters and/or numbers.

In contrast, arguments typically describe what a command should perform its action on. Arguments also follow the command, do not begin with a dash, and while typically appearing after options, may also be before or interspersed with options.

```
$ ls -l example/
total 112
-rw-r-----  1 oracle dba 24768 Oct 10 14:53 log1.log
-rw-r-----  1 oracle dba 24768 Oct 10 14:53 log2.log
-rw-r-----  1 oracle dba 24768 Oct 10 14:53 log3.log
-rw-rw-r--  1 oracle dba     0 Oct 10 14:10 output.txt
-rw-rw-r--  1 oracle dba     0 Oct 10 14:10 sample.txt
-rwxr-xr-x  1 oracle dba    96 Oct 10 14:51 test_script.sh
```

In this example, the command being called, *ls*, is modified with the *-l* option to cause it to return results with more detail than it normally does. The word *example/* is given as an argument causing *ls* to act on the *example* directory.

Some commands, like Oracle SQL*Plus require additional input beyond options and arguments. This type of input is usually prompted for once the command is running and entered interactively by the user.

When a command is covered in this book some of the commonly used options and arguments will be presented along with it. To learn more about a command you can consult the *man* page for that command by typing the *man* command with the command you want to learn about as an argument. How to view *man* pages will be covered in chapter 4.

Environmental variables can also modify the behavior of some commands. The next section will cover this in more detail, but a good example is how the setting of the ORACLE_HOME and ORACLE_SID variables affect what database the *sqlplus* command will connect to.

So, why all this talk about commands, options, arguments, and input? Well, all of these will be used in scripts and each requires some special handling. Options are fairly straightforward and can be simply applied to a command within a shell script. You will quickly discover that some commands will take only one argument while others will accept multiple, space separated arguments.

Interactive input is the most problematic to deal with in shell scripts since the application is typically expecting a human to be at the keyboard responding to output. Some tricks for dealing with all these will be presented in order to make shell scripts do as much work as possible for us.

Shell Variables

Shell variables give us a place to store values for use by the system, our shell, shell scripts, or by programs we run. Each session in UNIX has a set of variables that collectively are referred to as the environmental variables. These variables tell the system where to find applications and documentation, where the user's home directory is, the current working directory and much more. You can easily view all the environmental variables in the current session with the **env** command:

```
$ env
TERM=vt102
SHELL=/bin/bash
SSH_CLIENT=192.168.2.1 54620 22
OLDPWD=/export/home/oracle
SSH_TTY=/dev/pts/1
USER=oracle
MAIL=/var/mail//oracle
PATH=/usr/bin:/usr/ucb:/etc:.
PWD=/u01
TZ=US/Eastern
PS1=$
SHLVL=1
HOME=/export/home/oracle
LOGNAME=oracle
SSH_CONNECTION=192.168.2.1 54620 192.168.2.100 22
```

```
_=/usr/bin/env
```

These are some of the default variables provided by the system. As Oracle users, we are also familiar with shell variables such as *$ORACLE_HOME* and *$ORACLE_SID*.

While most of the environmental variables in the output above are set by the system, variables like *$ORACLE_HOME* need to be set by the user. In the Bourne and Bash shells, environmental variables are set by giving the variable name, the equal sign (=), and then the value to which the variable should be set. The variable must then be exported with the *export* command so it can become available to subsequent commands.

```
$ ORACLE_HOME=/u01/app/oracle/product/10.2.0/Db_1
$ export ORACLE_HOME
$ echo $ORACLE_HOME
/u01/app/oracle/product/10gR2/db_1
```

When setting variables you simply use the variable name; however, as shown in the above example, we use the *$* prefix to retrieve the value of a variable. You may also see the variable definition followed by the export on the same line separated by a semicolon. The semicolon marks the end of the first command allowing the commands to be executed as if they were on separate lines.

These exported environmental variables typically affect how UNIX and Linux behave or how other commands run. Though not a rule, environmental variable names are typically all uppercase. Lowercase variable names are typically used for local shell variables that are only needed in the current session or script. Local shell variables need not be exported.

```
$ day=Monday
$ echo $day
Monday
```

It is important to remember that shell variables are specific to a session, not a user. That means if you change the environment variables in one session it will not have any effect on other active sessions.

Beyond the familiar Oracle related shell variables we will be using shell variables for storing date information, file and directory names, passwords, and much more.

Conditions and if statements

Since the contents of variables will, well, vary, it is often useful to be able to make decisions based on them. Strings and numbers can be easily compared to explicit values or other variables. Here is a simple example:

```
$ i=107
$ if [ $i -gt 100 ]
> then
> echo "Wow, i got all the way up to $i"
> else
> echo "i is only up to $i"
> fi
Wow, i got all the way up to 107
$ i=22
$ if [ $i -gt 100 ]
> then
> echo "Wow, i got all the way up to $i"
> else
> echo "i is only up to $i"
> fi
i is only up to 22
```

Here we see a simple *if* statement. When executed the expression within the brackets is evaluated to either true or false. If the expression is found to be true the commands after the *then* will be executed, otherwise the commands after the *else* are executed.

The expression shown here is the greater than expression (>). The symbols we typically use for greater than and less than have specific significance in the UNIX shell, so to compare values we use *-gt* for greater than and *-lt* for less than. Comparisons can also be made between strings of text, but we will dig deeper into that in the chapter on Making Decisions.

Loops

While *if* statements let us make a command happen conditionally, loops will let us repeat the same command several times. In this simple example of a *while* loop we are just printing the loop counter *$i*. While this example does not do much work we will see later on that printing the loop counter can be a great help in troubleshooting problems with loops.

```
$ i=1
$ while [ $i -lt 10 ]
> do
> echo "The while loop counter is $i "
> i=`expr $i + 1`
> done
The while loop counter is 1
The while loop counter is 2
The while loop counter is 3
The while loop counter is 4
The while loop counter is 5
The while loop counter is 6
The while loop counter is 7
The while loop counter is 8
The while loop counter is 9
```

In this example we first set the variable *i* to 1. The *while* loop expression *$i -lt 10* is evaluated and as long as *i* is less than 10 and the commands between *do* and *done* are repeated.

The most important part of the *while* loop is the line *i=`expr $i + 1`*. This line takes the value of *i*, adds 1 to it and puts the resulting value back in the variable *i*. Without some change to the loop counter the *while* loop would continue to execute forever because *i* would never be increased to make it 10 or greater.

Later we will use *for* loops to automatically take a list and work through each item in it, but that will take a little more setup. For now just keep loops in mind as a way to easily achieve repeated tasks.

Wildcards and Pattern Matching

Wildcards provide a way to be less specific about what you are looking for in UNIX and Linux. This can be very helpful for acting on several similarly named files or directories at once, but wildcards must be used judiciously! It would be very easy to destroy or delete every file in a directory with a poorly placed wildcard.

The most popular wildcard is the * and is commonly referred to as star. When used in a command like the *ls* below it will match any number of occurrences, including zero, of any character. Let's say you want to look at every file in a directory with .txt in the name:

```
$ ls
log1.log        log3.log        sample.txt
log2.log        output.txt      test_script.sh
$ ls *.txt
output.txt   sample.txt
```

We can see that by using the * wildcard we can easily narrow down the files we will see without having to name them specifically. Less common but still quite useful is the ? wildcard. The ? wildcard will match zero or one occurrence of any character.

```
$ ls log?.log
log1.log   log2.log   log3.log
```

If you want to get even more specific and match one occurrence of only specific characters you can specify the characters to match within [] brackets.

```
$ ls log[2345].log
log2.log   log3.log
```

As shown in this example, the specified characters are evaluated individually so instead of matching the string *2345* the shell checks for the occurrence of each character individually and displays matching results. A range of characters can also be specified within brackets to look for any single character within that range. The following example will match the same files found by the previous one:

```
$ ls log[2-5].log
log2.log  log3.log
```

Ranges of letters can also be specified but it is important to remember that they will be case sensitive. For example the range *[a-z]* will match any lowercase character while the range *[A-Z]* will match any uppercase.

Finally the caret (^) may be used within brackets to match anything but the listed characters or range. In this example we will match any character except 2 through 5:

```
$ ls log[^2-5].log
log1.log
```

Wildcards can be combined in almost limitless ways to match groups of files but again, be careful! You want to be sure you're getting the right files and directories, no more, no less.

Relative and Absolute Paths

In the last chapter we talked a bit about how UNIX and Linux organize their files. Now we will take a closer look at how to reference specific files and directories.

The base of all UNIX and Linux directories is the / directory, typically referred to as 'slash' or the 'root directory'. From the /

directory we can very specifically name every other directory on the system. When a path is specified starting with / it is called an absolute path as it will point to the exact same directory regardless of the user's current directory.

As an example let's say we want to look at the directory we used when we were talking about wildcards. We know exactly where it is, so we can use the absolute path:

```
$ pwd
/home/oracle
$ ls /home/oracle/example/
log1.log  log2.log  log3.log  output.txt  sample.txt  test_script.sh
$ cd /tmp
$ ls /home/oracle/example/
log1.log  log2.log  log3.log  output.txt  sample.txt  test_script.sh
```

The *pwd* command, that stands for present working directory, shows that we are currently in the */home/oracle* directory. The *ls* works great from there, so to test the absolute path we change to the */tmp* directory and try the exact same command. Because we have specified the absolute path, the *ls* command still works.

A relative path is different as it specifies a location that is based on the current working directory. Relative paths may start with ./ or may just start with a directory name. Since relative paths refer to a directory or file's location relative to the current working directory we should not assume that a relative path will behave the same all the time.

```
$ cd /home/oracle
$ pwd
/home/oracle
$ ls example/
log1.log  log2.log  log3.log  output.txt  sample.txt  test_script.sh
$ ls ./example/
log1.log  log2.log  log3.log  output.txt  sample.txt  test_script.sh
$ cd /tmp
$ ls ./example/
ls: ./example/: No such file or directory
```

Here we see that if we are in the directory */home/oracle* we can list the contents of the directory *example* within that directory using a relative path with either the directory name or ./ prefix. When we change to another directory which doesn't have the *example* directory within it we see that the relative path fails to show us the directory we were looking for.

If we had changed our working directory to a directory where there was a different *example* directory we may have seen different results. Given the unpredictability of relative paths it is easy to assume that we should always use absolute paths but relative paths can be very useful when used properly. In certain applications, such as the *tar* utility, relative paths can actually be much safer than absolute paths.

Tilde, the Short Way Home

When files and directories exist within a user's home directory we can use a tilde (~) to refer to these without having to give an absolute path. If we want to refer directly to the current user's home directory, a tilde will suffice, but we can also prepend a tilde to a specific username to look in their home directory.

```
$ ls ~/example
log1.log  log2.log  log3.log  output.txt  sample.txt  test_script.sh
$ ls ~oracle/example
log1.log  log2.log  log3.log  output.txt  sample.txt  test_script.sh
```

Like with absolute paths, paths referring to home directories will refer to the same directory regardless of the current working directory, but keep in mind that if you do not specify the username, the tilde notation will behave differently depending on who uses it.

Permissions & Ownership

UNIX and Linux have very strict rules that allow each user to control who can view, modify, and execute their files. These rules allow multiple user and applications to work on the same system while maintaining security and privacy.

Every file and directory is owned by a single user. Each file and directory also has a security group associated with it that has access rights to the file or directory. If a user is not the directory or file owner nor assigned to the security group for the file, that user is considered other and may still have certain rights to access the file.

Each of the three file access categories, owner, group, and other, has a set of three access permissions associated with it. The access permissions are read, write, and execute.

A user may belong to more than one group. If permissions are granted on a file or directory to one of the user's groups they will be able to use the granted level of access, regardless of how many groups a user belongs to. You can check what groups a user is a member of with the *groups* command.

```
$ groups oracle
oracle : dba oinstall
```

In this case we see that the user *oracle* belongs to the groups *dba* and *oinstall*.

We can examine the permissions on a file with the *ls -l* command. This will print the permissions of each file in a directory. Permissions are represented in sets of three characters, *r* for read, *w* for write and *x* for execute, starting with the second character in the output. If a permission is not granted a dash (-) appears in its place.

Three of these sets will be displayed representing permissions granted to the owner, group and other users respectively.

```
$ ls -l
total 112
-rw-r-----  1 oracle dba 24768 Oct 10 14:53 log1.log
-rw-r-----  1 oracle dba 24768 Oct 10 14:53 log2.log
-rw-r-----  1 oracle dba 24768 Oct 10 14:53 log3.log
-rw-rw-r--  1 oracle dba     0 Oct 10 14:10 output.txt
-rw-rw-r--  1 oracle dba     0 Oct 10 14:10 sample.txt
-rwxr-xr-x  1 oracle dba    96 Oct 10 14:51 test_script.sh
```

On the files designated with the *.log* extension, the owner has read and write permissions, group has only read, and no permissions are assigned to other users. On *output.txt* and *sample.txt* the owner and group have read and write and other users only get read. Finally, on *test_script.sh* the owner has read, write and execute while the group and other users have only read and execute.

The execute permission on *test_script.sh* in this directory is important. That allows this file to be executed without using another program.

In this output we also see the owner of these files (*oracle*) and what group they belong to (*dba*) along with their size and when they were last modified.

File permissions, ownership, and how to set them will be covered later since these properties affect not only shell scripts, but every file the shell scripts touch.

Conclusion

In this chapter we have run through some of the key concepts that will be applied in shell scripting. We started off with a brief discussion on the various ways to connect to a UNIX or Linux system in order to access a shell including some tools you may find useful for connecting.

Since there are several possible shells to use we talked about how to tell what shell you are currently using. In case we want to use something other than the shell we are assigned at login, we saw how to switch shells on the fly.

While we have only discussed using a shell interactively, we touched on some of the differences we will encounter when we start using shell scripts in a non-interactive mode. Breaking down the structure of UNIX and Linux commands, we took a look at options, arguments, input, and how they must be handled.

We then delved into both environmental and user variables. Environmental variables control how the system and applications behave; user variables we can use entirely for our own purposes. Some uses for variables were demonstrated when we demonstrated *if* statements for making decisions and *while* loops for repeating actions.

Wildcards were shown as a way to work with multiple files at once. This can be quite powerful, however must be used with caution.

The two ways to refer to a file or directory, absolute and relative paths, were discussed. How absolute paths are a more specific way to refer to a file was covered, and we can often take advantage of relative paths for increased flexibility. The tilde (~) shortcut for referring to home directories was also presented.

We finished up by exploring how file and directory permissions are enforced and how they will affect our shell scripts. In the next chapter we will do some setup which will allow us to use the system more effectively.

Setting up your environment

You can do just about anything you want on a UNIX or Linux system without the need for any customization; however, a little time spent customizing your environment now will save you hours in the long run. In this chapter we will look at some of the things you may want to customize to make your environment more productive.

Configuring your default shell

So we have covered switching shells on-the-fly, but what if we want to permanently change our default shell? Well, depending on the breed of UNIX or Linux you are using, there will be different ways of changing a user's default shell. We will briefly discuss some of the more common methods here. You should consult your system administrator or operating system documentation to find out exactly how to change the default shell on your system.

Changing the Default Shell with usermod

While each operating system has its own set of tools, many include the *usermod* command. Unfortunately only the root user has privileges to use *usermod*.

Before you can use the *usermod* command you will need to know the full path to the shell you want to change to. You can find that with the *which* command, then to change the user's shell log into the system as root and call *usermod* as shown here:

```
# which bash
/bin/bash
# usermod -s /bin/bash oracle
```

The *which* command shows the full path to *bash* on this system as /bin/bash. This will vary between operating systems and versions. We then call *usermod* with the *-s* option. The full path to the bash shell is given directly after the *-s* option and finally we list the username whose default shell we want to change.

> 💣 Make sure you enter the full path to the shell correctly. If you make a typo or point to the wrong location for the shell the user will not be able to log in! This is especially important if you are changing the default shell for the root user.

If you do not have root privileges you will probably not be able to use the *usermod* command. To allow users to change their own shell, some systems have the change shell command that appears as *chsh*.

Changing Your Own Default Shell with the chsh Command

Some Linux and UNIX versions allow you to change your own shell with the *chsh* command. As with the *usermod* command, you will first want to look up the full path of the shell to which you wish to. Then to change the current user's default shell, simply type the *chsh* command and enter your password and desired shell when prompted.

```
$ which bash
/bin/bash
$ chsh
Changing shell for oracle.
Password: password
New shell [/bin/sh]: /bin/bash
Shell changed.
```

Regardless of how you make the change, changes to your default shell will not affect currently running sessions. Users must exit and re-initiate command line sessions to see their new default shell.

Entering a shell

When we connect to a system, we are automatically entered into our default shell. The last chapter covered a little about how we can then switch shells on the fly, but now let's take a closer look at what happens when we enter a shell.

Since we are mostly concerned with the Bourne and bash shells in this book we will focus on those here. While the startup behavior for most shells is similar, each will act a little differently when started. Most shells are well documented in their *man* page entries.

When bash is started as the default shell in a command line session, it will read a series of configuration files that can set environmental variables, change the prompt, set aliases, or even execute specific commands. Some of these files are shared between all the users on the system while others belong to a specific user.

bash Shell Login Behavior

The first file to be read and executed is */etc/profile*. This is the system wide configuration file and is always read by a login shell if it exists. The */etc/profile* file is typically maintained by the system administrator and should only contain settings and defaults applicable to every user on the system.

Next bash goes looking for one of the following files in the user's home directory:

- .bash_profile

- .bash_login

- .profile

The bash shell will read and execute the first of these files it finds and it looks in the order listed above. Once it has located and executed one of these startup files from the home directory all others will be ignored.

If none of these files were available, no environmental variables would be set and the user would have to type the full path to every command that is not internal to the shell. If bash goes looking for one of these files and it exists but is not readable it will report the error.

Since these files begin with a period (.) they will be hidden by default. If you want to view them in a directory listing you will need to use the *-a* option for the *ls* command.

With these startup files, it is important to remember that only the first one found will be read. If, for instance, you have both a .bash_profile and a .profile in your home directory, the .bash_profile is read and executed and the .profile ignored. For this reason we will only use the .profile startup file in this book.

Here is an example of a .profile startup file on Solaris:

```
#
# Copyright (c) 2001 by Sun Microsystems, Inc.
# All rights reserved.
#
# ident "@(#)local.profile     1.10    01/06/23 SMI"
stty istrip
PATH=/usr/bin:/usr/ucb:/etc:.
export PATH
PS1='$ '
```

```
export PS1
# Setup Oracle Variables
ORACLE_SID=oss
export ORACLE_SID
ORAENV_ASK=NO
export ORAENV_ASK
. oraenv
EDITOR=vi
export EDITOR
```

Within these files any text following a # is considered a comment and ignored. This allows us to annotate the startup files as we edit them to make their contents more meaningful.

In this profile we are taking advantage of the Oracle provided *oraenv* script to set some additional variables. By using the period ahead of the *oraenv* script, it is run in the same shell as the .profile rather than in a sub-shell. This allows variables to be set in the *oraenv* script, such as ORACLE_HOME and PATH, to take effect in the current environment.

The *EDITOR* variable seen here will affect what many applications will use when asked to edit text. SQL*Plus will call this command when the *edit* command is called at the SQL prompt.

If the same variable is set in both the /etc/profile and a startup file in your home directory, the one in your home directory will override the previously set variable. This allows users to override system defaults with their own settings.

With certain variables, such as PATH, we may want to use the system default but add more values to it. We will see how we can accomplish that later in this chapter.

If you want to invoke the bash shell in login mode without starting another command line session you can use the --login option.

```
$ bash --login
$ exit
```

This option causes bash to look for the exact same files it would if it had been started with a new command line session. This can be useful for testing changes to login scripts without continually having to log in each time. You can then type exit to return to your original shell session.

When bash is started interactively by typing *bash* at the command line but without the *--login* option it will look for a file called .bashrc in the current user's home directory. If it finds a .bashrc file it will execute it, but bash will not look for the other login files. Because the .bashrc file is not read by default at login we will make our changes to the .profile file and not use the .bashrc file.

Bourne Shell Login Behavior

The Bourne shell (*sh*) can be started as a login shell in the same ways bash can. The Bourne shell will also look for a */etc/profile* file, then a .profile in the current user's home directory. Bourne will not look for any other login files. If you are using a .profile file, it can be used for either bash or Bourne. This is one reason we have chosen to use .profile in our examples rather than .bash_profile or .login.

Non-Interactive Shell Behavior

When a shell is initiated non-interactively, as it will be by our shell scripts, it will not read any startup files. This means that environmental variables which are normally set in our startup files will need to be set within our shell scripts.

One way to work around this is to invoke the shell with the --login option. This will force the shell startup files to be read just as they are at login. If you do this, beware! By relying on variables set outside your shell script you are creating another point of failure. This can cause a shell script to stop working because someone changed his or her startup files. Additionally, another user may have a slightly different configuration than you, causing a shell script to work just fine for one person but not for another.

Setting Your Command Prompt

The command prompt you get when you connect to a command line session is highly customizable and everyone seems to want something different in it. In our examples we use one of the more common default prompts for the bash and Bourne shells, the dollar sign ($) but you should feel free to customize your prompt.

Basic Command Prompts

The prompt is set by defining the *PS1* shell variable. If you want the prompt to just contain text you can simply define it just like any other variable.

```
$ PS1=:
:PS1=': '
: PS1='Enter a command: '
Enter a command: PS1=$
$PS1='$ '
$
```

Changes to the PS1 variable will be seen immediately for the current session. In the example above we first set the prompt to a colon (:). We see on the next line that with just the colon our prompt is not separated from our command. To make the prompt more obviously separate from the command, we then set

PS1 to a colon with a space after it. To set a variable to a value with a space in it we enclose the value between double quotes. The space makes it a bit more clear where our prompt ends and our command begins.

Next we change our prompt back to the familiar dollar sign but now notice that the default prompt is not just a dollar sign but rather a dollar sign followed by a space, so we set PS1 to reflect that. While it is possible to set the prompt to nothing, I do not recommend it. Having your prompt blank makes it very hard to tell when a command has finished running.

When you get to a prompt you are happy with you can put the definition of it in your .profile file. Using your favorite text editor (such as vi) make a new line in your .profile file with the same *PS1='prompt'* that you used on the command line. Now every time you log in your prompt will automatically be set and ready to go.

Special Prompt Characters

bash allows several special characters to be used in a user's prompt which will then be expanded when the prompt is printed. These characters can be used in combination with text in the prompt but always begin with a backslash (\). Here are a few of the more useful special characters:

SPECIAL CHARACTER	DESCRIPTION
\d	The date spelled out in the form of "Weekday Month Date"
\@	The current time in 12 hour format with AM/PM
\u	The username of the current user
\h	The hostname of the system we are on
\w	The current working directory

Table 3.1: *Useful special characters*

Here are a few examples of how these special characters can be used in a prompt. Note that the prompt following the change represents the results of that change.

```
$ PS1='\d \@ $ '
Thu Oct 12 04:34 PM $ PS1='\u@\h$ '
oracle@sprog$ PS1='\w $ '
~ $ cd /usr/local
/usr/local $
```

The change directory (*cd*) command in this example is to demonstrate that the *w* character is showing the user's present working directory.

So you can start to see how the prompt can be customized to give feedback about the system, but the fun does not stop there! Commands and shell variables can also be used in command prompts.

Variables and Commands in Prompts

If you are not happy with any of the options so far, no need to worry, you can put almost anything in your prompt with shell variables and commands. Oracle administrators often want their current ORACLE_SID listed in their command prompt. This is easily accomplished:

```
$ PS1='$ORACLE_SID $ '
oss $
```

Be sure to use single quotes when enclosing variables and commands within the prompt. If you use double quotes, any variables or commands will be interpreted and substituted when the prompt is set but not be updated if the value changes during the session. By using single quotes the variables and commands will be substituted when the prompt is displayed. If, for instance, you change your ORACLE_SID variable to connect to a

---

different database, the new value for ORACLE_SID will be reflected in your prompt.

To use commands in the prompt, they must be enclosed between two grave symbols (`) more commonly called backquote or backtick in UNIX circles. Here is an example:

```
$ PS1='`uptime | cut -f 11-16 -d " "`$ '
 load average: 0.11, 0.07, 0.01$
```

Here we have set the PS1 prompt to show the current load average of the system by using the uptime and cut command. Everything within the backquotes is evaluated and the result substituted in the prompt. We then added "$ " to make it clear where the prompt ends.

I suggest keeping your prompt simple. Remember, whatever you put in there will be executed over and over while you are on the system. Most of the time I find username, hostname, and perhaps ORACLE_SID to be sufficient.

```
$ PS1='\u@\h $ORACLE_SID $ '
oracle@sprog oss $
```

A secondary prompt is used when entering commands on multiple lines. You will see this PS2 prompt when you enter a backslash (\) to continue a command on the next line. The default is usually good for this since you do not see it a lot, but if you wish to change it you can set the *PS2* environmental variable in the same way you would set PS1.

Prompts *PS3* and *PS4* can also be set but these are rarely seen. PS3 is used only in very specific shell syntax and PS4 is used when using a special trace option within the shell.

Setting Up the Binary Path

When you execute a command, like *ls* for instance, your shell goes looking for a command by that name in the directories specified in your PATH environmental variable. The PATH variable typically contains several locations separated by colons. When searching the path each directory is searched in order and the first command with the given name is executed.

To examine the current PATH variable we can echo its contents to the screen:

```
$ echo $PATH
/usr/kerberos/bin:/usr/local/bin:/bin:/usr/bin:/usr/X11R6/bin:/home/
oracle/bin
```

This shows a typical default PATH assignment. Based on this PATH on a typical system if the *ls* command is entered at the command line, the system would look for it first in */usr/kerberos/bin*, not finding it there it would then look in */usr/local/bin*. There is no command named *ls* there either so it would continue by checking in */bin* where it finds a command called *ls*. The system now executes the *ls* command found in the */bin* directory. The remaining directories in the PATH are never checked.

To determine where the system is finding a command without having to check each directory we can use the *which* command:

```
$ which ls
/bin/ls
```

This can be handy for troubleshooting when a command works for one user but not for another.

PATH is an environmental variable just like PS1. You can set PATH at the command line or make it persistent across logins by adding the definition to your .profile. You will also want to export the PATH variable after it has been set so the variable becomes available to scripts and other shells run by the current shell.

Typically, when making changes to the PATH variable, we do not want to completely replace the existing PATH, but instead want to add another directory to it. To do this, we can use the old PATH variable as part of its own definition.

As an example, let's say we have just installed some software in the /opt/bin directory. Now we want to make sure the new software is available for execution from the command line so we add it to the end of the PATH definition while using $PATH to fill in the current value for PATH.

```
$ echo $PATH
/usr/kerberos/bin:/usr/local/bin:/bin:/usr/bin:/usr/X11R6/bin:/home/
oracle/bin
$ PATH=$PATH:/opt/bin
$ export PATH
$ echo $PATH
/usr/kerberos/bin:/usr/local/bin:/bin:/usr/bin:/usr/X11R6/bin:/home/
oracle/bin:/opt/bin
```

If you wanted to make this change permanent you would now add the PATH definition and *export* of the PATH variable to your .profile file.

As with other environmental variables, if a change to the PATH needs to be made for all users on the system, you can make the change in the /etc/profile file. Each user can override the PATH in their own .profile but typically users just add to it with the method described above.

Many users choose to put an entry in their PATH for the current directory. This can be accomplished by having an empty entry, represented by either two colons next to each other or a colon at one end or the other, or by having the . directory in the PATH. Either way this has the effect of being able to run executables in the current working directory without having to use the ./ prefix.

This can be useful but may sometimes cause confusion. If you choose to do this, you will want to make sure you do not choose script names which are the same as commands on the machine, otherwise, depending on the search order, you may get one when you wanted another.

Some operating systems have very good default paths that require little modification. On others you will find yourself having to add several things to the path just to be able to work. You will also often need to add to the PATH when you add new software to the system. Most software will tell you where to find its binaries at install time. You can then check for that location in the PATH variable and add it if necessary.

The Manual Path

Another environmental variable that may need updating when new software is installed is the MANPATH variable. This variable is used by the *man* command that is used to display on-line manual pages for installed software. Similar to the PATH variable, MANPATH is made up of a colon-separated list of directories where on-line manual pages for software can be found.

When the *man* command is executed it expects a command name as an argument, for instance *man ls*. It will then check to see if the MANPATH environmental variable has been set. If it has not, man will look in the default manual directory, typically /usr/share/man. If the MANPATH environmental variable has been set, man will look through each directory listed in MANPATH in order until it finds a manual page that matches the command specified. If it does not find one it will report that "No manual entry for ls."

MANPATH is set in the same manner as PATH. It can be set at the command line, in a user's .profile or in the /etc/profile file for all users.

The Library Path

There may be times when installing or executing software that you are required to set an environmental variable such as LD_LIBRARY_PATH. This is to allow compilers and applications to find software libraries on the system.

While setting variables like LD_LIBRARY_PATH may help with the compilation of applications, setting this in the .profile or /etc/profile files should be avoided. While doing so may solve one problem, it is likely to cause another down the road. If you need to have LD_LIBRARY_PATH set to compile a certain application, simply set and export it in the current session. The required value for LD_LIBRARY_PATH will typically be found in install or support documentation for a product.

Aliases

Aliases are a great way to make shortcuts for long commands and make syntax more meaningful. When a command is typed at the command line, the shell will first check to see if there are any aliases for that command. If an alias has been defined for that word, the value of that alias gets executed instead of the command typed.

One way to use aliases is to make a word that is not normally recognized as a command do something. A common example of this is making an alias called *dir* which will list the contents of a directory. *dir* is the Microsoft DOS command to list the contents of a directory so having this alias can make DOS users feel more at home.

```
$ dir
-bash: dir: command not found
$ alias dir='ls'
$ dir
example        scripts        sqlnet.log
$ unalias dir
```

Here we see that before setting up the alias for *dir*, the command returns an error. We then use the *alias* command to set up an alias for dir to execute the *ls* command. Now we see that typing *dir* now lists the contents of the directory. To remove this alias we then use the *unalias* command.

Another common use of the *alias* command is to change the default behavior of a common command. A good application of this is with the *rm* command which means remove. By default rm will, if possible, remove files without any confirmation. This understandably makes many people uncomfortable, so a good alternative is to use the *-i* option which causes rm to prompt for confirmation on the removal of a file.

Here is how an alias can be used to change the default behavior of the *rm* command:

```
$ alias rm='rm -i'
$ rm log3.log
rm: remove log3.log (yes/no)? no
$ alias
alias rm='rm -i'
```

We see here how the syntax of the rm command stays the same but since the alias is substituting *rm -i* in place of *rm* at time of execution it causes rm to behave differently. We also see here that typing the *alias* command without any arguments will list all aliases currently set.

As with environmental variables, aliases can be set at the command line in a user's .profile or in the /etc/profile file. If an alias is set with the same name as an existing alias, the last one set will override the earlier alias.

Keeping your scripts organized

Keeping your scripts organized from the beginning can save a lot of confusion. While no two sites are the same here are a few guidelines I suggest for keeping your scripts organized.

- Keep your own user scripts in a directory named *scripts* within your home directory. This is a good place for scripts which only you will use or scripts which you are still developing.

- Optionally, add your user scripts folder to your PATH variable (~/scripts) so you do not have to type in the full path to your scripts when you want to execute them.

- Keep scripts which will be used on more than one Oracle database in a directory at *$ORACLE_BASE/common/scripts* or some other location which does not imply a specific database. This assumes you do not have a database named common.

- The common scripts directory could optionally be added to the PATH variable for individual users or all users.

- Scripts that are specific to a single database should be kept in a *scripts* folder within that database's *admin* folder.

- The scripts folders for individual databases should not be added to the PATH variable as it may cause scripts to be executed on the wrong database.

These are just guidelines. Do what makes sense at your site but make a point to make an active decision on where to keep your scripts, especially if more than one person will be developing or accessing them.

The .forward file

Some applications and scripts will send results and errors via email. Often these can be configured to send email directly to the pertinent users but another option is to have them sent to a system user and have them forwarded to the appropriate user through the use of a *.forward* file.

The .forward file, which is often referred to as 'dot-forward,' resides in a user's home directory. It is a plain text file which can contain one or more email addresses on separate lines. If your system is configured correctly, when mail is sent to a user who has a .forward file in their home directory the mail will automatically be forwarded to each user in the .forward file. The mail will not be kept on the system. Here is an example of what a typical .forward file might look like:

```
jon@lifeaftercoffee.com
dba@lifeaftercoffee.com
zach@lifeaftercoffee.com
```

If this were the .forward in the oracle user's home directory, any mail sent to oracle on this system would automatically be forwarded to all addresses listed and then it would be removed from the system.

Each operating system will need a slightly different setup to use .forward files and successfully forward email. Consult your system documentation if email is not being properly forwarded after the setup of a .forward file.

Default Permissions and umask

We touched on file permissions briefly in the last chapter, now we will look at how the default file permissions are set for a user.

When you create a file or directory, certain privileges are automatically assigned to it. For instance, the owner gets the privilege of reading from and writing to that file. Typically users with the same default group as you will also get read permissions on the file. On most systems, by default, all users will also get read permissions on the file you have created. The file mode creation mask or *umask* allows us to modify the default behavior to set appropriate default permissions on files. First we will go into a little more detail about file permissions then we will see how *umask* can be used to affect them.

File permissions are represented in two ways, by letters corresponding to permissions and by a sum of numbers that correspond to permissions. Here is a chart of the numbers and letters and the permissions they represent:

PERMISSION	NUMERIC REPRESENTATION	CHARACTER REPRESENTATION
Read	4	r
Write	2	w
Execute	1	x

Table 3.2#: *File permissions*

As an example, the character representation for read, write and execute would be *rwx*. The numeric representation would be the sum of 4, 2 and 1 so the numeric representation for read, write and execute would be 7. The character representation for read and execute would be r-x and the numeric would be 5, the sum of 4, 0, because there is no write permission, and 1.

Since we need to represent permissions for the owner, group, and other users on the system these permissions are typically represented in sets of three. When viewing a detailed directory listing we see the character representation of the permissions for the owner, group and other users listed in that order.

```
$ ls -l
total 112
-rw-r-----  1 oracle dba 24768 Oct 10 14:53 log1.log
-rw-r-----  1 oracle dba 24768 Oct 10 14:53 log2.log
-rw-r-----  1 oracle dba 24768 Oct 10 14:53 log3.log
-rw-rw-r--  1 oracle dba     0 Oct 10 14:10 output.txt
-rw-rw-r--  1 oracle dba     0 Oct 10 14:10 sample.txt
-rwxr-xr-x  1 oracle dba    96 Oct 10 14:51 test_script.sh
```

The umask comes into play when creating files and directories. When a user creates a new file, the permissions will be read and write, minus whatever permissions are represented in the umask. To view the current umask value simply type *umask* without any parameters.

```
$ umask
0022
$ touch myfile.txt
$ ls -l myfile.txt
-rw-r--r--  1 oracle dba 0 Oct 13 18:24 myfile.txt
```

The *umask* command shows that the current umask is 0022. The first number of the output represents some advanced permissions which we will not delve into right now. The remaining numbers show us that no permissions should be masked from the file owner and write should be masked from the group and other user on the system. When we create an empty file with the *touch* command we see that the file was indeed created with read and write permissions for the owner and read-only for the group and other users. By default, files are not created with execute permissions so there are no execute permissions granted to anyone.

Now we will change our umask to allow others in the group to write to this file while making it so other users who are not in this group cannot read the file.

```
$ umask 006
$ touch anotherfile.txt
$ ls -l anotherfile.txt
-rw-rw----  1 oracle dba 0 Oct 13 18:35 anotherfile.txt
```

Here we see how the change in umask has resulted in a change in new file permissions. By removing write (2) from the group portion of the mask, other users in this group can now write to this file. We also see that by adding read (4) to the original write (2) in the mask for other users, we have now made it so other users on the system who do not have the group indicated in the file permissions will not have any permissions on the file.

The umask setting of 006 seems like it should result in permissions equivalent to 771 granting all rights to user and group and execute to other. That would be the case, except there is a system wide umask of 111 which is applied to files. The combination of these two umasks results in the equivalent of 660 granting read and write to user and group and no permissions to other users.

Default directory permissions are determined in the same way except the execute (1 or x) permission is granted by default. The execute permission on a directory controls whether a user can change directories into the indicated directory. As such it is fairly harmless so can typically be left on by default.

When setting up your umask it is useful to see what the resulting permissions will be without having to create a test file or directory to test it. To view what the resulting permissions of your current umask will be, you can call the umask command with the -S option.

```
$ umask -S
u=rwx,g=rwx,o=x
```

To make a change in the umask persistent between sessions, you can add the umask command to your .profile file.

Conclusion

After this chapter, hopefully you are comfortable with customizing your environment to make you more productive.

We have covered configuring your default shell so you will be in your preferred shell when you start a session and how to enter another shell when you need to. The startup files which bash will run, if present, were covered and many of the options presented in the rest of the chapter can be configured in these startup files.

One of the most popular ways of customizing your environment is changing the prompt. We reviewed how to change it to have text, special prompt characters, variables, and commands in it.

We explored quite a bit the PATH environmental variable and how it is used to locate commands typed on the command line. The manual page path and library path were also examined.

Aliases were shown as a way to have a custom way to call a command. We also showed how to use aliases to change the default behavior of a command by creating an alias with the same name.

Script organization will become very important as we get more scripts so some recommendations for organizing your scripts were given. We then covered how a .forward file can be used to send emails to addresses off the system.

Finally we examined in depth the umask and how it is used to determine default file permissions.

In the next chapter we are going to get right into using some of the tools provided by UNIX and Linux, but you should keep this chapter in mind as you move forward. Consider what you want to see in your prompt, what aliases might be useful, and what directories you may need to add to your PATH.

Key tools

In this chapter we are going to have a look at some of the most useful and important commands and tools available in Linux and UNIX. Now I am sure I have left out some people's favorite tools, but what is presented here should be enough to get someone off to a good start.

man - The Online Manual Pages

Typically when a command is installed on Linux or UNIX some documentation is installed with it. The *man* command allows you to view the documentation, typically called man pages, right from the command line.

We have already mentioned the *man* command a couple times to find out more information about specific commands. *man* can be called with a command as the argument.

```
$ man ls
Reformatting page.  Please Wait... done

User Commands                                              ls(1)

NAME
     ls - list contents of directory

SYNOPSIS
     /usr/bin/ls [-aAbcCdeEfFghHilLmnopqrRstuvVx1@] [file...]

     /usr/xpg4/bin/ls          [-aAbcCdeEfFghHilLmnopqrRstuvVx1@]
     [file...]

     /usr/xpg6/bin/ls          [-aAbcCdeEfFghHilLmnopqrRstuvVx1@]
     [file...]
```

```
For each file that is a directory, ls lists the contents  of
the  directory.  For  each file that is an ordinary file, ls
repeats its name and any other  information  requested.  The
output is sorted alphabetically by default. When no argument
is given, the current  directory  is  listed.  When  several
arguments   are   given,  the  arguments  are  first  sorted
appropriately, but file arguments appear before  directories
...
```

The man pages are good for looking up options to commands, but they can quickly become overwhelming. For instance, in the output of the *man ls* above, you can see all the potential options for the *ls* command: *-aAbcCdeEfFghHilLmnopqrRstuvVx1@*. Of all these options you will probably only ever use a few of them and trust me, the options in man pages are not listed in order of popularity.

Another major downfall of the man pages is they typically do not include examples. The combination of all these factors makes it difficult to learn a new tool through just man pages but they still make a great secondary reference, especially for options.

So when you want to learn more about the commands presented in this chapter, or you find yourself needing information on a command not presented here, try using the *man* command.

Text Editors

Command-line and Graphical Editors – In Brief

In this book we will primarily use the command-line editor *vi*. *vi* was chosen for this book largely because it can be found on nearly every modern Linux and UNIX system. It does not need to be installed or configured — it is just there.

Some may prefer to do their shell scripting in a graphical text editor. If that is your preference, go ahead. Many modern text editors like EditPlus (editplus.com) offer syntax highlighting for shell scripts. By highlighting keywords, syntax highlighting will make it easier to read and debug your scripts. Just make sure the editor you choose does not add any markup, like MS Word and Rich Text editors do, and watch for options like UNIX style line breaks and set them appropriately.

My recommendation is that even if you intent to do most of your shell scripting in a graphical editor, you should learn a bit of vi. That way when you need to make a quick change to a shell script or a system file you do not need to go through the effort of downloading it to your local machine, making the change, then moving it back.

vi - The Visual Editor

You may not believe me at first, but *vi* is one of the most powerful text editors around. Several books available on vi explore the potential of the editor more deeply, but for now we will try to get enough familiarity with vi to be able to confidently get around.

Invoking vi

vi is typically started with a file name as an argument. If you are editing an existing file you would use either the relative or absolute path and file name. You will then see the beginning of the file you are editing.

```
$ vi test_script.sh
#!/bin/sh
i=1
while [ $i -lt 10 ]
do
echo "The while loop counter is $i "
i=`expr $i + 1`
done
~
~
~
~
```

Oracle Shell Scripting

```
~
~
~
~
~
~
~
~
~
~
~
~
~
"test_script.sh" 7L, 96C                                        1,1
All
```

If you wanted to make a new file you can start *vi* with a new file
name as an option. In this case you will see a blank screen in *vi*.

```
$ vi new_script.sh

~
~
~
~
~
~
~
~
~
~
~
~
~
~
~
~
~
~
~
~
"new_script.sh" [New File]                                      0,0-1
All
```

In both of these cases we see that *vi* uses the tilde character (~) to
represent lines past the end of the file you are editing. That is so
you can tell blank lines from lines which are not part of your file.

You can start *vi* without giving a filename. That will start vi with a new file which you can then name when you save. While there are several options for *vi,* you will probably find that you rarely need them. Most of the magic of vi happens by using commands within the editor.

Switching Modes

As far as day-to-day usage goes, *vi* has two modes, *insert* and *command.* Insert mode allows you to enter text into your file while command mode lets you perform operations like searching, saving, moving around the file, and quitting vi. When you initially start *vi* you will be in command mode.

There are several ways to go from command to insert mode depending on what you want to do and where you want to do it. The escape key is the preferred way to go from insert mode to command mode. Here are a few common ways to switch modes:

COMMAND	ACTION
i	Insert text to the left of the cursor position
a	Insert text to the right of the cursor
I	Insert text at the beginning of the current line
A	Insert text at the end of the current line
o	Start inserting on a new line below the current line
O	Start inserting on a new line above the current line
escape	Return to command mode

Table 4.1: *Common commands for entering and exiting insert mode*

It is important to note that these commands are case sensitive. Typically the upper-case version of a command has a similar effect to the lower-case version but it is never exactly the same.

When in doubt about your mode the safest thing to do is press the escape key. That will always return you to command mode.

Moving Around

While in command mode you can typically use the arrow keys to move around a file. If the arrow keys are not working, which is typically due to a problem with terminal emulation, you can still get around using the h, j, k and l keys. While it may seem tedious to use these keys, they offer a needed substitute for when the arrow keys are not working.

Beyond using these substitutes there are also several other ways to more efficiently move the cursor around in vi. Here are some of the most useful commands for moving around:

COMMAND	ACTION: MOVE THE CURSOR
←, →	left or right one character
↑, ↓	up or down one line
h	left one character
l	right one character
j	down one line
k	up one line
$	to the end of the current line
^	to the beginning of the current line
w	to the beginning of the next word
b	to the beginning of the previous word
G	to the end of the file
25G	to line 25 (any number can be used instead of 25)
enter	to the beginning of the first word on the next line

Table 4.2: *Cursor movement commands*

You might notice that adding a number before the *G* command changes its behavior. Many vi commands can be preceded with a number to affectively execute the command that number of times. For example, the command *8↓* would move the cursor down eight lines, just as if the down arrow were pressed eight times. Similarly *5w* would move the cursor to the beginning of the word five words to the left.

Making and Undoing Changes

There are several ways to make changes in vi. Some will delete or change a single character while others work on an entire word or row. Like the others, you will need to be in command mode to use these commands. Here are some common commands for making changes to text in vi:

COMMAND	ACTION
x	Delete one character
r	Replace one character with the next character typed
dw	Delete from the cursor position to the end of the current word
dd	Delete the current line
D	Delete from the current character to the end of this line
cw	Same as dw then enter insert mode
cc	Clear the text on this line and enter insert mode
C	Delete from the current cursor position to the end of the current line and enter insert mode
J	Join the next line to the current line
u	Undo the last change. Can be repeated to undo the past several changes.

Table 4.3: *Commands for changing text and undoing changes*

Many of these commands can be preceded with a number to repeat the command that number of times. Even the undo (*u*) command can be preceded by a number to undo several changes at once.

Copying and Pasting

vi offers many options for copying and pasting including the ability to copy and paste from multiple buffers, but we will just touch on the basic copy and paste commands. A buffer is similar to the clipboard in MS Windows or Mac OS. The following commands will allow you to copy and paste one or more lines:

COMMAND	ACTION
yy	Copy the current line into the default buffer
7yy	Copy the current line plus the next six lines to the default buffer
p	Paste the contents of the default buffer below the current line
P	Paste the contents of the default buffer above the current line

Table 4.4: *Common copy and paste commands*

If you copy multiple lines with the *yy* command you do not have to specify the number of lines when pasting. The paste command will automatically paste the entire contents of the default buffer.

Searching and Replacing

Searching for text and replacing text in *vi* can be very handy but it is not as easy as you might think! Here are some of the more useful search and replace commands in vi:

Command	Action
/*search text*	Find and move the cursor to the next occurrence of *search text*
?*search text*	Find and move the cursor to the previous occurrence of *search text*
n	Repeat the last search
N	Repeat the last search but in the opposite direction (previous occurrence instead of next or next occurrence instead of previous)
:%s/*search text*/*replace text*/g	Find all occurrences of *search text* and replace it with *replace text*

Table 4.5: *Some search and replace commands*

When these commands encounter the end of the file they will wrap around to the beginning and continue searching. If searching backwards they will wrap from the beginning to the end. You probably noticed the find and replace command is very complicated. There are ways of making it even more complicated and having it search only specific lines, but you will not typically need that level of complexity.

Saving and Exiting

You will want to save your work often and when you are done you will need to get out of *vi*. As with other things in vi, there are several ways to save and exit. Here are a few common ones:

COMMAND	ACTION
:w	Save changes
:w *filename.txt*	Save changes to *filename.txt* instead of the file we opened
:q	Exit vi (changes should have already been saved
:q!	Exit vi without saving changes
:wq	Save changes and exit vi
ZZ	Save changes and exit vi (same as :wq)
:w!	Write changes despite read-only permissions (must be file owner)

Table 4.6: *Commands to save and exit vi*

Remember, this short section is just a starting point. This should be enough vi for you to get around and do some shell scripting. Nothing is hard to do in *vi* although it will be hard to remember at first. Like anything, the more you use *vi* the better you will get at it.

Manipulating Text

We will spend a lot of time manipulating text in our shell scripts. Sometimes we will be trimming down output to give the user more meaningful feedback, sometimes we will be making decisions based on a string in the output, and sometimes we will be making commands based on text. Here we are looking at the basic commands we will be using to manipulate text.

Searching with grep

grep is a fairly simple utility with the sole purpose of checking a file for a given pattern of text. By default *grep* will print out all lines of the file which contain the given text.

The *grep* command typically takes two arguments, the string of text to search for followed by the file or files to search.

```
$ grep 'operating system' types_of_unix.txt
UNIX is a group of computer operating systems.
Unlike Microsoft Windows there are several companies who make UNIX
operating systems but they must all comply with the "Single UNIX
Specification" and be certified as such in order to be called UNIX.
Many more operating systems are UNIX-like.
Of these UNIX-like operating systems Linux is by far the most
prominent.
```

Here we see every line containing the string 'operating system' in the file types_of_unix.txt. It is important to note that unless the *−i* option is specified the character matching for *grep* is case sensitive.

We can specify multiple files by either listing multiple files after the expression or by using a wildcard to match multiple files as shown in the example below.

```
$ grep do *
test_script.sh:do
test_script.sh:done
types_of_unix.txt:Just like Microsoft Windows it controls the
computer hardware, does it's best to keep all your devices playing
nicely together and gives you an interface to run things on the
computer.
types_of_unix.txt:Unlike Microsoft Windows there are several
companies who make UNIX operating systems but they must all comply
with the "Single UNIX Specification" and be certified as such in
order to be called UNIX.
```

Here we see that *grep* matched one line with the word *do* on it, but also matched a line with the word *done* which contains the letters *do*.

When *grep* is used against multiple files it will automatically prefix each matching line of output with the name of the file it found that in.

grep has several useful options.

OPTION	EFFECT
-c	Print only the count of the number of lines the pattern was found on. When used with multiple files the name of all files checked will be printed followed by the number of lines the pattern was found on in that file.
-h	Prevents the file name from being printed when checking multiple files
-i	Ignore the case of text and match any occurrence of the pattern
-l	Print only the name of each file which contains the pattern
-n	Show the line number before printing lines containing the pattern
-v	Print every line that *doesn't* contain the given pattern

Table 4.7: *Some common options for the grep command*

These are the options you are most likely to use. Keep in mind that many options can be combined to give you just the results you want. Also remember that *grep* will count the number of lines with a pattern on them, not the number of occurrences of that pattern, so if the pattern occurs twice on the same line, *grep — c* only counts that as one.

More Complex Searches with egrep

egrep lets you get a lot more sophisticated than *grep* by specifying a more complex expression. *egrep* has similar syntax and results to grep but uses *regular expressions* which allow you to match characters, ranges of characters, strings and by combining options you can search for just about anything else you'd find in text.

We are not going to get too deep into regular expressions. Like *vi*, regular expressions could be a book by themselves. When we use them in scripts I'll describe how each regular expression works, but to give you an idea we will look at a few examples.

The pipe (|) character in a regular expression allows you to search for one string or expression *or* another also matching lines which contain both. This egrep command will search for every line containing the string *while* or the string *do*.

```
$ egrep 'while|do' ./test_script.sh
while [ $i -lt 10 ]
do
echo "The while loop counter is $i " while
done
```

egrep also allows you to specify a range of characters, either letters or numbers, to match any line which contains characters within that range.

```
$ egrep '[0-9]' ./test_script.sh
i=1
while [ $i -lt 10 ]
i=`expr $i + 1`
$ egrep '[A-Z]' ./test_script.sh
echo "The while loop counter is $i " while
```

Like *grep*, *egrep* is case sensitive. In the second example above *[A-Z]* matches all upper-case letters.

With *egrep* and *regular expressions* you can search for very complex patterns of characters. Here we have just touched on some very simple examples. As you can imagine *regular expressions* quickly become difficult to understand but when used properly can be very powerful.

---

sed Text Substitution

sed has a little different function than *grep* and *egrep*. Not only will *sed* identify occurrences of a pattern of characters, but upon reading a file it can make editing changes to that file and then output the entire text of the changed file. Like *egrep* this is probably better understood through example.

```
$ more types_of_unix.txt
UNIX is a group of computer operating systems.
Just like Microsoft Windows it controls the computer hardware, does
it's best to
 keep all your devices playing nicely together and gives you an
interface to run
 things on the computer.
Unlike Microsoft Windows there are several companies who make UNIX
operating sys
tems but they must all comply with the "Single UNIX Specification"
and be certif
ied as such in order to be called UNIX.
Some popular versions of UNIX are Solaris, AIX, HP-UX and Tru64.

Many more operating systems are UNIX-like.
These systems meet many, or possibly even all of the characteristics
specified i
n the single UNIX specification, however have not been certified.
Of these UNIX-like operating systems Linux is by far the most
prominent.
Conversationally Linux is often referred to as UNIX, though it is
not currently
certified as such.

The information about UNIX in this book can all be applied to Linux
except where
 specifically noted.
$ sed -e 's/UNIX/Unix/g' types_of_unix.txt
Unix is a group of computer operating systems.
Just like Microsoft Windows it controls the computer hardware, does
it's best to keep all your devices playing nicely together and gives
you an interface to run things on the computer.
Unlike Microsoft Windows there are several companies who make Unix
operating systems but they must all comply with the "Single Unix
Specification" and be certified as such in order to be called Unix.
Some popular versions of Unix are Solaris, AIX, HP-UX and Tru64.

Many more operating systems are Unix-like.
These systems meet many, or possibly even all of the characteristics
specified in the single Unix specification, however have not been
certified.
Of these Unix-like operating systems Linux is by far the most
prominent.
```

```
Conversationally Linux is often referred to as Unix, though it is
not currently certified as such.

The information about Unix in this book can all be applied to Linux
except where specifically noted.
```

In the above example we first examine the contents of the text file *types_of_unix.txt* with *more*. We then use *sed* to change every occurrence of 'UNIX' to 'Unix'. The *−e* option tells *sed* to execute the commands given as the following argument, in this case 's/UNIX/Unix/g'. In this particular *sed* command the *s* tells *sed* to substitute, UNIX is given as the original string, Unix is given as the string to put in place, and the *g* causes this change to be applied globally.

This simplest usage of *sed* can be very powerful for changing database SIDs in a script, altering a path which is repeated in a script, or just about anything else where you want to do a quick text replacement.

sed can also be used to simply delete a pattern of text. In this slightly more complicated *sed* command we use a couple regular expressions, similar to what we used with *egrep*, to search for and remove lines which do not contain any text.

```
$ sed -e '/^$/d' types_of_unix.txt
UNIX is a group of computer operating systems.
Just like Microsoft Windows it controls the computer hardware, does
it's best to keep all your devices playing nicely together and gives
you an interface to run things on the computer.
Unlike Microsoft Windows there are several companies who make UNIX
operating systems but they must all comply with the "Single UNIX
Specification" and be certified as such in order to be called UNIX.
Some popular versions of UNIX are Solaris, AIX, HP-UX and Tru64.
Many more operating systems are UNIX-like.
These systems meet many, or possibly even all of the characteristics
specified in the single UNIX specification, however have not been
certified.
Of these UNIX-like operating systems Linux is by far the most
prominent.
Conversationally Linux is often referred to as UNIX, though it is
not currently certified as such.
The information about UNIX in this book can all be applied to Linux
except where specifically noted.
```

In the command '/^$/d' sed will search for any line which the newline character (represented here by the caret) is followed directly by the end of the line (represented by the dollar sign.) The *d* command tells *sed* to delete all occurrences of this pattern and we see the blank lines have been removed from the output.

These are only the simplest examples of how we can use *sed*, but they are also some of the most common. In scripts where more complicated *sed* commands are used, we will explain exactly what is going on. Here we saw how the results of the *sed* editing are written to the standard output (the screen) but later we will see how we can redirect this output to go to another file instead.

Breaking Out Columns with cut

cut is a useful command for manipulating files which are organized into columns. For example, let's say we have a text file which is the output of a SQL*Plus selection from the *dba_users* table. The output has three columns, but we are only really interested in the first. Here is how we can apply the *cut* command to get just the first column:

```
$ more accounts.txt
SQL> select username, account_status, created from dba_users;

USERNAME                      ACCOUNT_STATUS                   CREATED
----------------------------- -------------------------------- ---------
MGMT_VIEW                     OPEN                             12-JUL-05
SYS                           OPEN                             12-JUL-05
SYSTEM                        OPEN                             12-JUL-05
DBSNMP                        OPEN                             12-JUL-05
SYSMAN                        OPEN                             12-JUL-05
OUTLN                         EXPIRED & LOCKED                 12-JUL-05
WMSYS                         EXPIRED & LOCKED                 12-JUL-05
ORDSYS                        EXPIRED & LOCKED                 12-JUL-05
EXFSYS                        EXPIRED & LOCKED                 12-JUL-05
XDB                           EXPIRED & LOCKED                 12-JUL-05
DMSYS                         EXPIRED & LOCKED                 12-JUL-05

USERNAME                      ACCOUNT_STATUS                   CREATED
----------------------------- -------------------------------- ---------
OLAPSYS                       EXPIRED & LOCKED                 12-JUL-05
SI_INFORMTN_SCHEMA            EXPIRED & LOCKED                 12-JUL-05
ORDPLUGINS                    EXPIRED & LOCKED                 12-JUL-05
MDSYS                         EXPIRED & LOCKED                 12-JUL-05
```

```
CTXSYS                  EXPIRED & LOCKED              12-JUL-05
ANONYMOUS               EXPIRED & LOCKED              12-JUL-05
MDDATA                  EXPIRED & LOCKED              12-JUL-05
TSMSYS                  EXPIRED & LOCKED              12-JUL-05
DIP                     EXPIRED & LOCKED              12-JUL-05
SCOTT                   EXPIRED & LOCKED              12-JUL-05

21 rows selected.

SQL> spool off
$ cut -f1 -d" " accounts.txt
SQL>

USERNAME
------------------------------
MGMT_VIEW
SYS
SYSTEM
DBSNMP
SYSMAN
OUTLN
WMSYS
ORDSYS
EXFSYS
XDB
DMSYS

USERNAME
------------------------------
OLAPSYS
SI_INFORMTN_SCHEMA
ORDPLUGINS
MDSYS
CTXSYS
ANONYMOUS
MDDATA
TSMSYS
DIP
SCOTT

21

SQL>
```

Here we used the *cut* command and specified the *–f1* option to output only the first field. A tab character is the default delimiter that *cut* will look for but instead here we use the *–d* option to tell *cut* to delimit based on the space character. This is also a good example of where we might then want to apply another command like *grep* or *sed* to narrow down our results even further.

Another way to use the *cut* command is on character position instead of columns. With the same file we used in the last example we may want to grab the username and created date. Since there are multiple spaces between the columns using the space as a delimiter will not work. Instead we can use the *-c* option to specify exactly which characters we want to grab from each line.

```
$ cut -c1-30,60-74 accounts.txt
SQL> select username, account_status, created from dba_users;

USERNAME                       CREATED
------------------------------ ---------
MGMT_VIEW                      12-JUL-05
SYS                            12-JUL-05
SYSTEM                         12-JUL-05
DBSNMP                         12-JUL-05
SYSMAN                         12-JUL-05
OUTLN                          12-JUL-05
WMSYS                          12-JUL-05
ORDSYS                         12-JUL-05
EXFSYS                         12-JUL-05
XDB                            12-JUL-05
DMSYS                          12-JUL-05

USERNAME                       CREATED
------------------------------ ---------
OLAPSYS                        12-JUL-05
SI_INFORMTN_SCHEMA             12-JUL-05
ORDPLUGINS                     12-JUL-05
MDSYS                          12-JUL-05
CTXSYS                         12-JUL-05
ANONYMOUS                      12-JUL-05
MDDATA                         12-JUL-05
TSMSYS                         12-JUL-05
DIP                            12-JUL-05
SCOTT                          12-JUL-05

21 rows selected.

SQL> spool off
```

Here we have grabbed characters 1 through 30 and characters 60 through 74 of each line. In this way we can use *cut* to trim down files to just the parts that we want. This comes in very handy when we are given preformatted output which does not meet our needs.

Using awk to Find Just What You Need

awk is a powerful text manipulation tool. While *awk* supports many features of a programming language, such as variables and functions, in shell scripts it is frequently used to execute short programs to perform specific text manipulation.

In our scripts *awk* is most useful when looking for a piece of text within certain context. The *awk* command can take several options and expects two arguments, the *awk* commands to be executed and the file on which to perform them.

We can use *awk* to search for and print lines containing certain text, like we do with *egrep* using the following syntax:

```
$ awk "/OPEN/" accounts.txt
MGMT_VIEW                       OPEN                         12-
JUL-05
SYS                             OPEN                         12-
JUL-05
SYSTEM                          OPEN                         12-
JUL-05
DBSNMP                          OPEN                         12-
JUL-05
SYSMAN                          OPEN                         12-
JUL-05
```

Here the *awk* command interprets the expression OPEN, although more complex regular expressions are acceptable, and performs only on the lines which contain that expression. Since no additional action was specified *awk* performs the default action of printing each line found.

awk can also be used much like the *cut* command to print certain columns. In the following example we build on the previous *awk* command by telling it to print only column 1, represented by $1.

```
$ awk "/OPEN/ {print \$1}" accounts.txt
MGMT_VIEW
SYS
SYSTEM
DBSNMP
SYSMAN
```

This overrides the default behavior of printing each line and causes *awk* to return only the first column of lines which contain the text OPEN. The backslash (\) in front of the $1 variable prevents it from being interpreted as a shell variable.

Here is an example of how *awk* is used in Oracle's *dbhome* script. *dbhome* is called by *oraenv*.

```
$ awk -F: "/^oss:/ {print \$2; exit}" /etc/oratab
/u01/app/oracle/product/10.2.0/db_1
```

Without getting too much into the context of the *dbhome* script, this simple *awk* script is used to find and print the second column of the */etc/oratab* entry for the *oss* database. That column indicates what the ORACLE_HOME variable should be set to for a specific database.

This command uses the *-F* option to indicate that the colon character should be used as the separator instead of spaces or tabs. The expression */^oss:/* causes *awk* to only act on lines which contain the text *oss:* directly after the newline which is represented by the caret.

awk will then perform the operations indicated between the curly brackets on each line. In this case the operations are to print column 2 and exit. The exit is significant as it causes *awk* to quit after processing the first line, assuring that only one entry will be returned.

awk commands can get very complicated but offer another way to hone in on the information we are looking for. *awk* supports many more commands and options and I will make a point to explain *awk* commands as they are used in the scripts in this book.

Sort - Get Things in Order

The *sort* command can be used to quickly sort text alphabetically or numerically. Using the same text file as we did in the past few examples we can show how *sort* can order the output alphabetically.

```
$ sort accounts.txt
```

```
--------------------------- ------------------------------- ---------
--------------------------- ------------------------------- ---------
21 rows selected.
ANONYMOUS                   EXPIRED & LOCKED                12-JUL-05
CTXSYS                      EXPIRED & LOCKED                12-JUL-05
DBSNMP                      OPEN                            12-JUL-05
DIP                         EXPIRED & LOCKED                12-JUL-05
DMSYS                       EXPIRED & LOCKED                12-JUL-05
EXFSYS                      EXPIRED & LOCKED                12-JUL-05
MDDATA                      EXPIRED & LOCKED                12-JUL-05
MDSYS                       EXPIRED & LOCKED                12-JUL-05
MGMT_VIEW                   OPEN                            12-JUL-05
OLAPSYS                     EXPIRED & LOCKED                12-JUL-05
ORDPLUGINS                  EXPIRED & LOCKED                12-JUL-05
ORDSYS                      EXPIRED & LOCKED                12-JUL-05
OUTLN                       EXPIRED & LOCKED                12-JUL-05
SCOTT                       EXPIRED & LOCKED                12-JUL-05
SI_INFORMTN_SCHEMA          EXPIRED & LOCKED                12-JUL-05
SQL> select username, account_status, created from dba_users;
SQL> spool off
SYS                         OPEN                            12-JUL-05
SYSMAN                      OPEN                            12-JUL-05
SYSTEM                      OPEN                            12-JUL-05
TSMSYS                      EXPIRED & LOCKED                12-JUL-05
USERNAME                    ACCOUNT_STATUS                  CREATED
USERNAME                    ACCOUNT_STATUS                  CREATED
WMSYS                       EXPIRED & LOCKED                12-JUL-05
XDB                         EXPIRED & LOCKED                12-JUL-05
```

We see here that even blank lines and symbols are sorted. By default, *sort* orders the lines by the ASCII character order. It is important to remember that in ASCII the upper-case letters A-Z come before the lower-case letters a-z which will cause upper-case *Z* to come before lower-case *a*. The *-f* option can be used to change the behavior of *sort* to sort both upper and lower-case letters as if they were upper-case resulting in a case-insensitive sort.

By default *sort* evaluates numbers first on the leading character, then on the second, and so on. This results in, for instance, the number *11* being sorted before the number *2*, because the *sort* command starts off only taking the first character into consideration. The *−n* option can be added to cause the *sort* command to properly represent numbers.

View the Beginning or End of a File

Sometimes we are only concerned with what is at the very beginning or very end of a file. Two tools are provided to help us with these circumstances, *head* and *tail*.

head takes a file name as an argument and by default will show you the first 10 lines of that file.

```
$ head log1.log
4Suite-1.0-8.b1.i386.rpm
GConf2-2.10.0-4.i386.rpm
ImageMagick-6.2.2.0-2.i386.rpm
MAKEDEV-3.19-1.i386.rpm
MyODBC-2.50.39-24.i386.rpm
MySQL-python-1.2.0-1.i386.rpm
NetworkManager-0.4-15.cvs20050404.i386.rpm
ORBit2-2.12.1-3.i386.rpm
PyXML-0.8.4-3.i386.rpm
SDL-1.2.8-3.2.i386.rpm
```

If you want to see more or less of the file you can specify how many lines you want to see as an option to *head*. Here we see *head* used to view only the first 5 lines of the file *log1.log*.

```
$ head -5 log1.log
4Suite-1.0-8.b1.i386.rpm
GConf2-2.10.0-4.i386.rpm
ImageMagick-6.2.2.0-2.i386.rpm
MAKEDEV-3.19-1.i386.rpm
MyODBC-2.50.39-24.i386.rpm
```

tail works almost exactly like *head* but instead prints the last lines of a file.

```
$ tail log1.log
xscreensaver-base-4.21-4.i386.rpm
xsri-2.1.0-9.i386.rpm
xterm-200-6.i386.rpm
yp-tools-2.8-8.i386.rpm
ypbind-1.17.2-5.i386.rpm
yum-2.3.2-7.noarch.rpm
zip-2.3-30.i386.rpm
zlib-1.2.2.2-3.i386.rpm
zlib-devel-1.2.2.2-3.i386.rpm
zsh-4.2.1-2.i386.rpm
```

tail can also be used with an option to specify how many lines to see, but an even more interesting option to *tail* is the *-f* option. With the *-f* option tail will print the last ten lines of the file but instead of stopping there it keeps the file open and will print any new lines as they are written to the file.

```
$ tail -f log1.log
xscreensaver-base-4.21-4.i386.rpm
xsri-2.1.0-9.i386.rpm
xterm-200-6.i386.rpm
yp-tools-2.8-8.i386.rpm
ypbind-1.17.2-5.i386.rpm
yum-2.3.2-7.noarch.rpm
zip-2.3-30.i386.rpm
zlib-1.2.2.2-3.i386.rpm
zlib-devel-1.2.2.2-3.i386.rpm
zsh-4.2.1-2.i386.rpm
control-c
```

Tail will continue following the file until it is cancelled by typing *control-c*. This is very useful for following changes to a file or keeping up with the log to another application.

Counting Characters, Words and Lines with wc

Sometimes we do not care about the contents of a file so much as we may need to know how many lines, words, or characters are in it. For this we can use the *wc* (word count) command.

```
$ wc types_of_unix.txt
  11 156 961 types_of_unix.txt
$ wc -l types_of_unix.txt
11 types_of_unix.txt
$ wc -w types_of_unix.txt
```

```
156 types_of_unix.txt
$ wc -m types_of_unix.txt
961 types_of_unix.txt
```

The default output of the *wc* command, which is shown first, displays the number of lines, words and characters respectively followed by the file name that was counted. If you want to get more specific you can add the *-l* option to only display the number of lines, the *-w* option to only display the number of words, or the *-m* option to display only the number of characters in the file.

wc will be useful for examining the size of logs, counting files in a directory, and checking the number of running processes. We will use it often to provide this type of summary information.

Managing Processes

Every time we run a command, the shell starts that command as a child process. The command runs under its own process ID number (PID), performs its function, and exits, ending the child process. If everything goes right the user will get their shell prompt back and can then execute their next command. Of course, sooner or later everything will not go right. When that happens you will need some of the following tools to seek out and end the process manually.

Stopping the Current Process

When you run a command or script from the command line you know the command has completed when you get your prompt back. If the command is taking longer than expected, or you suspect there may be a problem with the command which will cause it not to finish, or not to finish soon, you can usually stop that process by typing *control-c*.

After typing *control-c* you should get your prompt back and you should check the results of the command you were running. The command may have worked properly and have been just about to finish, it may have worked only partially, or it may have done nothing at all.

Finding and Stopping Other Processes

Sometimes a stubborn command will not respond to a *control-c* or you may need to stop a command run by another user or started by the system. In these instances the first step is identifying the right process to kill.

Viewing running processes with ps

The *ps* command is used to view the process status of processes currently running on the system. Without options, *ps* will print information about processes started by your current session.

```
$ ps
  PID TTY          TIME CMD
13452 pts/3    00:00:00 bash
13612 pts/3    00:00:00 ps
```

Here we see the *bash* command running as our current shell and the *ps* command which we were executing to examine the running commands. The default output for the *ps* command shows four things. The first column shows the process ID (PID) of the running commands. The next column shows the terminal, if any, that the command was associated with. The time that the command has spent on the CPU is displayed in the third column, and the fourth column shows the command which is running.

To see more details on the running processes we can add the *-f* flag to the *ps* command.

```
$ ps -f
UID         PID  PPID  C STIME TTY          TIME CMD
oracle    13452 13451  0 15:06 pts/3    00:00:00 -bash
oracle    13924 13452  0 15:45 pts/3    00:00:00 ps -f
```

The *-f* option adds a few useful things to the output including the user ID (UID) of the person running that command, the parent process ID (PPID) and the starting time of the process (STIME). You will also find that instead of just listing the command under the CMD column, that *ps* is now listing the command, options and arguments which were given for that command.

There are two commonly used options which allow you to see processes other than those started by the current shell session. The *-e* option will output every processes running on the system regardless of who owns it. This is often a large list, but here is a partial output of the *ps -ef* command:

```
$ ps -ef
UID         PID  PPID  C STIME TTY          TIME CMD
root          1     0  0 13:10 ?        00:00:01 init [5]
root          2     1  0 13:10 ?        00:00:00 [ksoftirqd/0]
root          3     1  0 13:10 ?        00:00:00 [watchdog/0]
root          4     1  0 13:10 ?        00:00:00 [events/0]
root          5     1  0 13:10 ?        00:00:00 [khelper]
root          6     1  0 13:10 ?        00:00:00 [kthread]
root          8     6  0 13:10 ?        00:00:00 [kacpid]
root         64     6  0 13:10 ?        00:00:00 [kblockd/0]
...
oracle     2945     1  0 13:18 ?        00:00:00 /usr/libexec/gconfd-2 14
oracle     2946  2903  0 13:18 ?        00:00:00 kio_file [kdeinit] file
/tmp/kso
oracle     3038  2903  0 13:18 ?        00:00:03 /usr/bin/autorun -l --
interval=1
oracle     3081  2935  0 13:23 ?        00:00:00 /usr/bin/kdesktop_lock
oracle     3082  3081  0 13:23 ?        00:00:00 kpartsaver.kss -window-id
314572
root       3848     1  0 14:16 ?        00:00:00 cupsd
root      13446  2164  0 15:06 ?        00:00:00 sshd: oracle [priv]
oracle    13451 13446  0 15:06 ?        00:00:00 sshd: oracle@pts/3
oracle    13452 13451  0 15:06 pts/3    00:00:00 -bash
oracle    14006 13452  0 15:54 pts/3    00:00:00 ps -ef
```

The *-f* option typically accompanies the *-e* option to show the user ID of the user running the process.

It is important to note here that any user can view any other user's running processes complete with options and arguments! Because of this it is important that we not include passwords or any other important information when we call a command. If we do, it could be exposed to other users!

The other option which can be useful for tracking down processes is the *-u* option. This option allows you to specify which user's processes you wish to see. Here is a partial output of the Oracle user's running processes:

```
$ ps -fu oracle
    UID   PID  PPID  C    STIME TTY        TIME CMD
 oracle  2066  2064  0 12:24:49 pts/1      0:01 -bash
 oracle  2064  2061  0 12:24:49 ?          0:02 /usr/lib/ssh/sshd
 oracle  2079     1  0 12:29:57 ?          0:01
/u01/app/oracle/product/10.2.0/Db_1/bin/tnslsnr LISTENER -inherit
 oracle  2199     1  0 12:31:57 ?          0:09 ora_pmon_oss
 oracle  2201     1  0 12:32:00 ?          0:01 ora_psp0_oss
 oracle  2203     1  0 12:32:00 ?          0:01 ora_mman_oss
 oracle  2205     1  0 12:32:00 ?          0:03 ora_dbw0_oss
 oracle  2207     1  0 12:32:01 ?          0:04 ora_lgwr_oss
 oracle  2209     1  0 12:32:02 ?          0:10 ora_ckpt_oss
 oracle  2211     1  0 12:32:02 ?          0:08 ora_smon_oss
 oracle  2213     1  0 12:32:03 ?          0:00 ora_reco_oss
 oracle  2215     1  0 12:32:03 ?          0:20 ora_cjq0_oss
 oracle  2217     1  0 12:32:04 ?          0:10 ora_mmon_oss
 oracle  2219     1  0 12:32:04 ?          0:18 ora_mmnl_oss
...
 oracle  2740  2527  0 14:56:21 pts/3      0:00 ps -fu oracle
```

Another option *-U* will allow you to view processes based on who called them. We will see in a later chapter how we can get a script to execute as someone other than the person who called it, but since this feature is somewhat rarely used you will usually want to use the *-u* option when searching for processes by user.

 In some operating systems, (especially those based on BSD), the *-f* flag does not exist and *-e* is for environment, not every user. To get similar output on these systems you need to do *ps –aux*.

Ending running processes with the kill command

When all else fails and a command will not respond to normal ways of shutting it down, like a stubborn database process which does not die after the database is shut down, the *kill* command can be used to tell the command to shut down.

The *kill* command sends a signal to the given process. The process will try to catch this signal and respond appropriately.

To send a signal to a running process you will first need its process ID. That is usually found using the *ps* command as described above. Once you have the process ID you should first try sending a SIGTERM to the process. No options are needed to send the SIGTERM, so all we have to do is run the *kill* command with the process ID as an argument:

```
$ kill 2205
```

This command sends a SIGTERM signal to process number 2205. If the process is working properly it will catch the SIGTERM signal, clean up and release system resources and shut down. If things go well this should not take more than a few seconds so we can check for the process again in say five or ten seconds and see if it has shut down.

If that does not do the job we can send a slightly more urgent SIGINIT signal to the process. To do that we add the *-2* option to the *kill* command.

```
$ kill -2 2205
```

The SIGINIT signal still relies on the process we are signaling catching the signal, cleaning up, and then shutting down. This also should only take a couple seconds at most. So if we check back and the process is still there, we will need to take stronger actions.

The last resort is to send the SIGKILL signal to the process. SIGKILL cannot be trapped by the process we are signaling but rather causes the process to die without performing any cleanup. To send the SIGKILL we use the *-9* option.

```
$ kill -9 2205
```

Since no cleanup is done, the *kill -9* happens almost immediately. Also, since a SIGKILL is not interpreted by the process there may be system resources such as temp files, allocated memory, and network sockets still allocated by the now deceased process.

Performing a *kill -9* is equivalent to pulling the plug on the system without the benefit of a clean restart to clear memory and system resources. They should be avoided when possible, but will inevitably be necessary sometimes.

The *kill* command, along with the *pkill* command we will cover shortly can only be used to signal processes owned by the current user. The one exception to this is that the root user has the ability to use the *kill* command against any user's processes.

pgrep and pkill

The *pgrep* and *pkill* commands offer another way to search for and send signals to processes. *pgrep* allows you to search for a command using a pattern of characters which are in the command executed or using the *-u* option in the same way it can be used with the *ps* command. The major difference with the *pgrep* command is it will report back only the process ID of processes found suppressing all other information.

```
$ pgrep lsnr
2079
```

Here we have used *pgrep* to look for any process with the pattern *lsnr* in the command. *pgrep* returns the process ID which we could then use with the *kill* command, but *pkill* offers us another option.

The *pkill* command uses the same method of matching processes as the *pgrep* command, but instead of returning the process ID it will automatically send a signal to the matched process in the same way the *kill* process does.

Just like the *kill* command, *pkill* will send a SIGTERM signal if no option is specified.

```
$ pkill lsnr
```

The *-2* and *-9* options for SIGINIT and SIGKILL respectively are also valid with *pkill* and have the same affect on processes matched.

> Great caution must be taken when using the *pkill* command! It is very easy to signal the wrong process and you will not be warned or given any feedback by pkill! For this reason I recommend using the *ps* command to identify processes then using the *kill* command with the appropriate process ID.

Examining how long a command takes

Sometimes it is useful to know exactly how long a command takes to run. To get a very accurate timing of a command we can use the *time* command. *time* is an unusual command as it takes another command as an argument. Here is an example:

```
$ time dbstart
Processing Database instance "oss": log file
/u01/app/oracle/product/10.2.0/Db_1/startup.log
```

```
real    0m55.770s
user    0m0.348s
sys     0m0.798s
```

time returns three numbers. The first, labeled *real* represents the amount of time between when the command was started and when it completed. This is sometimes referred to as *wall clock time*. The second and third numbers represent how much time the command spent executing as the current user and how much time it spent executing at the system-level.

The sum of the user and system times can be considered how much processor time this command took. Since the system is always performing multiple tasks the total processor time will typically be much less than the real time.

time can be a great way to identify what methods are most efficient for performing a task or comparing the execution time of a command while another variable is changed.

Job Control - Running Jobs in the Background

If you need to execute a time consuming command and do not want to wait for it to complete to continue with your shell session, you can use the ampersand (*&*) character after a command to background the process. When you use this method to run commands in the background, the shell will report back the job number in brackets and the process number of the background process.

```
$ dbstart &
[1] 2142
$ Processing Database instance "oss": log file
/u01/app/oracle/product/10.2.0/Db_1/startup.log

$
```

Here we see that we receive our prompt back allowing us to execute other commands, but we still see the output of this command written to the terminal. Things can become very confusing if we have a bunch of background processes writing to our terminal so it is best to background processes with little or no output or redirect the output to a file or other resource. Redirecting output will be covered later in this chapter.

Anyway, now that we have a process running in the background we might want to know when it completes. The shell will typically report a "Done" message with the job number when a process completes, but if you want to check what is going on in the meantime you can use the *jobs* command to check the status.

```
$ jobs
[1]+  Running                 dbstart &
```

jobs will report back the job number, status, and command for any processes currently running or stopped in the background. The status is indicated as *Running* if the process is running in the background, *Stopped* if the process is waiting for input or has been stopped with the *control-z* command or *Done* if the process has just finished running.

If a process is started normally, without an ampersand, and you find you need to either pause the execution or would rather the process run in the background instead of canceling the process and restarting it with an ampersand, you can use the *control-z* command to stop the process and manipulate the job from there.

```
$ dbshut
control-z
[1]+  Stopped                 dbshut
$ jobs
[1]+  Stopped                 dbshut
$ bg 1
[1]+ dbshut &
$ jobs
[1]+  Running                 dbshut &
```

Once the job is stopped it will show up in the job list with a status of *Stopped*. To start the job executing in the background you can use the *bg* command with the job number. As seen above, this changes the status to *Running* and the job will continue to run as if it were started with an ampersand.

Whether a job is stopped or running in the background, it can be brought back to the foreground with the *fg* command. This allows you to interact with the program just as if it was started normally. Plus, you will get your prompt back when the command completes or you get tired of waiting and background it again with the *control-z* command.

```
$ dbstart &
[1] 2599
Processing Database instance "oss": log file
/u01/app/oracle/product/10.2.0/Db_1/startup.log

$ jobs
[1]+  Running                 dbstart &
$ fg 1
dbstart
$
```

Here is a table that can be used as a quick reference for these job control commands. Job control can allow you to get multiple things running at once, but watch out for commands which might interfere with each other and make sure you can keep track of the output.

COMMAND	ACITON
&	Append to the end of a command to start it running in the background
jobs	Display all backgrounded jobs whether running or stopped
control-z	Stop the job running in the current shell and background it
bg 1	Start running a job 1 in the background
fg 1	Move job 1 to the foreground, moving it into the current shell

Table 4.8: *Job Control Commands*

Making sure things keep running with nohup

When you exit a command line session or if you lose your connection for some reason, the system automatically sends all the processes you had running in that session a SIGHUP signal. The SIGHUP signal could also be sent with the *kill* command in the same way we sent other signals.

The SIGHUP signal is interpreted by the processes and normally will cause them to shut down and die. To prevent this and allow a command to continue running after logout or session failure you can add the command *nohup* before the command to be executed.

```
$ nohup vmstat 30 10 &
[1] 4708
Sending output to nohup.out
$ exit
```

In this example we are calling the *vmstat* command with arguments that cause it to gather statistics on the use of system resources 10 times waiting 30 seconds between each execution. Since we used the *nohup* command the output from the command is automatically redirected to a file called *nohup.out*. The *nohup.out* file is created in the present working directory when the *nohup* command is called so if the shell session is interrupted we can still pick up the output.

We also used an ampersand in this execution so we would immediately get our prompt back to continue working in this shell. Now we can exit this shell and reconnect with a new command line session and examine the *nohup.out* file for the results.

```
$ more nohup.out
 kthr      memory            page            disk          faults      cpu
 r b w   swap  free   re  mf pi po fr de sr dd dd f0 s1   in   sy   cs us sy id
 0 0 0 492872 67664    4  23 15  4  7 4792 8 3  1  0  0  408   94  172  1  3 96
 0 0 0 399168 13120    4  28 162 0  0  0  0  2 17  0  0  439   91  199  1  2 97
```

```
0 0 0 397760  7192  11  64  88 15 15   0   0   2 10  0  0  428  229  203  1  3 96
0 0 0 399504  7488  70  75 707 36 63 0 16 12   7  0  0  440  190  196  3  4 93
0 0 0 399064  6048   3  17  15 33 41   0   7   3  3  0  0  414   65  178  1  2 98
0 0 0 399848  6728   6  54  66 17 17 248 1   5  2  0  0  416   96  179  1  2 97
0 0 0 399024  5976   2   4   5 16 17   0   0   2  2  0  0  410   83  176  1  2 98
0 0 0 399776  6584  11  63  11 14 16 1208 1 2   1  0  0  408  123  176  1  2 97
0 0 0 399032  5928   2   0   0 16 16   0   0   2  1  0  0  408   59  170  0  1 98
0 0 0 399560  6952  14  78 299 149 183 2088 96 15 1 0 0 433  402  194  9  3 87
```

nohup is useful when you know a command will take a long time and suspect it might be interrupted for some reason such as auto-logout, network issues, or desktop power failure. *nohup* can also be applied to a command which is already running. By calling *nohup -p* with a process ID number as an argument, you can force that process to ignore the SIGHUP signal.

```
$ vmstat 30 10 &
[1] 4760
 kthr      memory            page              disk          faults      cpu
 r b w   swap  free  re  mf pi po fr de sr dd dd f0 s1   in   sy   cs us sy id
 0 0 0 492144 67208   4  23 15  4  7  0  8  3  1  0  0  408   94  172  1  3 96

$ nohup -p 4760
Sending output to nohup.out
```

We see that applying the *nohup* even after the command has started will cause the output of the command to be redirected to the file *nohup.out*.

File and Directory Ownership and Permissions

UNIX and Linux security relies heavily on file ownership and permissions to determine who can do what. Proper permissions and both user and group ownership must be maintained to set up and assure that a system will continue running properly.

In chapter 2 introduced the types of permissions and explored how to view the permissions and ownership of files with the *ls -l* command. Now we are going to look at how to change the owner, group, and permissions on files.

Managing the owner and group of a file

The *chown* and *chgrp* commands are used to manipulate the owner and group of a file respectively. To maintain security, most changes to file ownership must be done as root.

chown expects two arguments. First you list the username of the user who you wish change the ownership to, then the file name.

```
# ls -l accounts.txt
-rwxrwxrwx   1 oracle   oinstall     2069 Oct 29 12:36 accounts.txt
# chown jemmons accounts.txt
# ls -l accounts.txt
-rwxrwxrwx   1 jemmons  oinstall     2069 Oct 29 12:36 accounts.txt
```

chgrp works very similarly to *chown* but, of course, you supply a group name instead of a user name as the first argument. To change the group of a file you must have write permissions on the file and be a member of the group you wish to change the file to.

```
$ groups
oinstall dba
$ ls -l nohup.out
-rw-------   1 oracle   oinstall     1655 Oct 31 15:26 nohup.out
$ chgrp dba nohup.out
$ ls -l nohup.out
-rw-------   1 oracle   dba          1655 Oct 31 15:26 nohup.out
```

The root user is needed if you want to change the group of a file to a group that the owner does not have.

There is a shortcut for changing both owner and group with the same command. You can use the *chmod* command and supply a username and group separated by a colon followed by a file name to change both simultaneously.

```
# ls -l nohup.out
-rw-------   1 oracle   dba          1655 Oct 31 15:26 nohup.out
# chown jemmons:other nohup.out
# ls -l nohup.out
-rw-------   1 jemmons  other        1655 Oct 31 15:26 nohup.out
```

This will also usually require root privileges since you are changing the ownership of the file.

Managing File Permissions

In the Key Concepts chapter information was presented on how different permissions, such as read, write and execute, can be granted at different levels, such as owner, group and other, in order to control access to files and directories. These permissions are controlled by the *chmod* command.

There are several methods for using *chmod*. In the most straightforward method we will give *chmod* two arguments, first a string of characters which indicate the permission change and then the file or directory to which we want to apply the change.

```
$ ls -l test_script.sh
-rwxr-xr-x  1 oracle dba 102 Oct 22 14:53 test_script.sh
$ chmod o-x test_script.sh
$ ls -l test_script.sh
-rwxr-xr--  1 oracle dba 102 Oct 22 14:53 test_script.sh
$ chmod g+w test_script.sh
$ ls -l test_script.sh
-rwxrwxr--  1 oracle dba 102 Oct 22 14:53 test_script.sh
$ chmod o=rx test_script.sh
$ ls -l test_script.sh
-rwxrwxr-x  1 oracle dba 102 Oct 22 14:53 test_script.sh
```

Here the first *chmod* command uses the minus symbol (-) to remove the execute permissions from other users who are not the owner or part of the group to which this file belongs. The second uses a plus (+) to grant the write privilege to users in the group to which this file belongs. The third *chmod* command uses an equal sign (=) to set the permissions for other to read and execute, effectively removing the write permission if it had been granted.

Here are the common symbols used for defining permissions with the *chmod* command.

PRIVILEGE GROUP INDICATOR	MEANING	CHANGE INDICATOR	MEANING	PRIVILEGE INDICATOR	MEANING
U	user	+	add permission	r	read
g	group	-	remove	w	write
o	other	=	update to this permission	x	execute

Table 4.9: *Character symbols for permission modification*

To the left of the change indicator (+, - or =), you can give multiple permission levels to be affected. For example, *go+w* would grant write to the group and other users. To the right of the change indicator you can also provide more than one privilege to affect as we saw in the example above. If desired more than one set of changes can be combined in the same command by separating them with a comma like in the following example:

```
$ chmod u=rwx,g=rx,o= test_script.sh
$ ls -l test_script.sh
-rwxr-x---  1 oracle dba 102 Oct 22 14:53 test_script.sh
```

Permissions can also be specified using a number designation. When using this method three numbers are typically given which stand for, in order, the user, group, and other permission. The numbers range from 0 to 7 and have the following meaning:

NUMBER	AFFECTIVE PERMISSION
0	---
1	--x (not typically used)
2	-w- (not typically used)
3	-wx (not typically used)

NUMBER	AFFECTIVE PERMISSION
4	r--
5	r-x
6	rw-
7	rwx

Table 4.10: *chmod numeric designations*

Each of these numbers is derived from the sum of the three permissions where read is represented by 4, write by 2 and execute by 1. For instance, read and write, without execute would be 4 (read) + 2 (write) = 6. As mentioned above, these numbers are used in groups of three to represent user, group and other permissions.

```
$ chmod 754 test_script.sh
$ ls -l test_script.sh
-rwxr-xr--  1 oracle dba 102 Oct 22 14:53 test_script.sh
```

This usage of *chmod* allows all three permissions to be set simultaneously and absolutely so, although the numbers are more difficult to remember they are commonly used.

How Permissions Affect Directories

Directory permissions are changed in the same method as file permissions but the results can be rather surprising and sometimes confusing.

To examine the permissions on a directory you will want to use the *-ld* option for the *ls* command. This will show the properties of the directory rather than listing its contents. Here we see the typical directory permissions:

```
$ ls -ld example/
drwxr-xr-x  2 oracle dba 4096 Oct 29 22:38 example/
```

On directories, the *read* permission controls the ability to list the contents of a directory. By removing the read permission from our example we see that we no longer can list the contents of the directory:

```
$ chmod u-r example/
$ ls example/
ls: example/: Permission denied
$ cd example/
$ pwd
/home/oracle/example
$ ls
ls: .: Permission denied
```

Even after changing directory into *example* we cannot list the contents, however it is significant that we can *cd* into the directory.

The *write* permission on a directory will control whether a user, group, or other users can create or delete a file or subdirectory of a directory, however the *execute* permission has the unexpected behavior of controlling if a user can *cd* into a directory. To demonstrate we will replace the read permission and remove execute on our example directory.

```
$ cd ../
$ chmod u+r example
$ chmod u-x example
$ ls example/
anotherfile.txt  log2.log  myfile.txt  sample.txt
types_of_unix.txt
log1.log         log3.log  output.txt  test_script.sh
$ cd example/
-bash: cd: example/: Permission denied
```

We see here that after removing the execute privilege we can list the contents of the directory however we cannot *cd* into it. If you wish to make a directory viewable to other users it is best to share both the read and execute privileges so users can both list and *cd* into the directory.

There are three advanced options for permissions, the *setuid*, *setgid* and *sticky bit* options. The *sticky bit* is not really used much any more but on shared directories affectively locks files within the directory from being modified by users other than the file creator. This is how the /tmp directory is typically maintained since multiple users require access to it. The *setuid* and *setgid* permissions offer a way to control what user scripts are executed as and will be discussed in detail in a later chapter.

Securing Important Files

On a multi-user system, like most UNIX and Linux systems, there will likely be some information you wish to keep from other users. Often shell scripts may have passwords in them or you may have documents or directories which other users should not see. The best way to secure these files and directories while still maintaining access to them yourself is to use the *chmod* command to remove all permissions from group and other users.

```
$ ls -l test_script.sh
-rwxr-xr-x  1 oracle dba 102 Oct 22 14:53 test_script.sh
$ chmod go-rwx test_script.sh
$ ls -l test_script.sh
-rwx------  1 oracle dba 102 Oct 22 14:53 test_script.sh
```

This modification will assure that this file cannot be viewed, modified, or executed by any other user on the system. Assuming others do not have your username and password, this makes it safe to keep secure data like passwords on the system. This will be necessary for some of our scripts which require passwords.

> Do not change the permissions on installed software unless you *really* know what you are doing. A few improper permission changes on files in the ORACLE_HOME directory could quickly render Oracle unusable.

Manipulating Input and Output

Up until now we have been using the keyboard for input and our terminal session (screen) for output. UNIX and Linux allow for several other options including reading files as input, writing to files as output, and even using one command as input or output for another.

Redirecting Standard Input

When you call a command which requires you to enter text the command is typically looking for that text on *standard input* which under most circumstances is your keyboard. Additionally, many commands which we have been using file names as arguments will default to using standard input if no file is specified. The *sort* command offers a good example of this.

sort can take text directly from the standard input and sort it.

```
$ sort
Groucho
Harpo
Chico
Zeppo
control-d
Chico
Groucho
Harpo
Zeppo
```

When using a command in this manner *control-d* is used to indicate the end of input. We see here that *sort* has given us the lines that we typed on the standard input but sorted alphabetically.

Now, if instead of using the keyboard for input we want to use a file, we can use a less-than sign (<) between the command and a filename. Note that the command should come first when redirecting input.

In this example I have created the text file *marx.txt* with *vi*. We then use the less-than sign to redirect the file to the standard input of *sort*.

```
$ more marx.txt
Groucho
Harpo
Chico
Zeppo
$ sort < marx.txt
Chico
Groucho
Harpo
Zeppo
```

In this example *sort* would commonly be used on text, however we will see that in some cases we will redirect binary files to commands which can handle them.

This method works well if the desired input is already in a file on your system. If the input is not already in a file, it is possible to redirect input from the command line or more likely a script to a command. To redirect input from the command line a double less-than sign is used followed by a file marker.

```
$ sort << EOF
> Groucho
> Harpo
> Chico
> Zeppo
> EOF
Chico
Groucho
Harpo
Zeppo
```

In this case the file marker *EOF* is used but any contiguous string of characters not broken by whitespace could be used. The shell will read input from the command line or script until it encounters a line which contains only the file marker. After the end file marker is found all the input will be sent to the command just as if it were coming from a file.

We will see this method used with several commands, especially *sqlplus*. This will enable us to have the functionality achieved by having an input file without needing to maintain a second file in order for our script to work.

Multiple file markers can be used within a single script, however they should all be unique. When using multiple file markers it is common to use EOA, EOB, EOC etc. or EOF1, EOF2, EOF3 etc. Using a file marker which is in all capitol letters makes it easy to spot the file markers in a script but is not necessary.

Redirecting Standard Output and Standard Error

Until this point all the output we have been seeing from commands has been printed to the screen. There are two types of output we have been seeing, *standard output* and *standard error* output. By default, both of these are printed to the screen; however, we can redirect the output from either or both to files.

For simplicity we will use the *ls* command for this example. Normally *ls* prints the contents of the directory to the screen. If we want to make a file with the directory listing we can easily redirect the output of *ls* with the greater-than symbol (>).

```
$ ls
log1.log   log3.log   myfile.txt   sample.txt        types_of_unix.txt
log2.log   marx.txt   output.txt   test_script.sh
$ ls > listing.txt
$ more listing.txt
listing.txt
log1.log
log2.log
log3.log
marx.txt
myfile.txt
output.txt
sample.txt
test_script.sh
types_of_unix.txt
```

You might have noticed that when printing to the screen *ls* printed more than one file name per line; but, when the output was redirected to the file it prints only one file per line. *ls* will only print multiple items per line when printing to the screen unless specified to do otherwise.

This simple method redirects the *standard output* to the file *listing.txt*. If the file *listing.txt* already exists, it will be overwritten! If you want to append output to the same file without overwriting the current contents you can use two greater-than symbols in place of the one (>>). This has the affect of creating an ongoing log with the newest additions always at the bottom.

But what about *standard error*? When redirecting *standard output* with either the > or the >> symbols, errors will still be printed to the screen as can be seen at the beginning of the example below. This is often useful, but if you want to redirect errors to a file as well, we can do that too.

```
$ ls notthere.txt > listing.txt
ls: notthere.txt: No such file or directory
$ ls notthere.txt > listing.txt 2> error.txt
$ more error.txt
ls: notthere.txt: No such file or directory
```

We see in this example that the *ls* command has failed because we asked it to list a file that does not exist. The error is printed to the screen even though the standard output has been redirected to a file. We then take and redirect *standard error*, represented by the number 2, to the file *error.txt*. We now see nothing is printed to the screen; however, when we examine the *error.txt* file we see the text of our error there.

As mentioned above, the *standard error* output is represented by the number *2*. That is its file descriptor or the number the system is using to access the file. *Standard input* and *standard output* also have numeric file descriptors: *standard input* is known to the system as *0* and *standard output* as *1*, but with the redirect commands presented above the use of the numbers is unnecessary.

It is possible to redirect both input and output simultaneously. We will often see this with *sqlplus* when taking input from a script and sending the output to a file.

audit_locked_accounts.sh (partial script shown)

```
sqlplus -S "/ as sysdba" << EOF > /tmp/audit_locked_accounts_oss.txt

    set pagesize

    select 'The following accounts were found to be unlocked and
should not be'
    from dual;

    define exit_status = 0

    column xs new_value exit_status

    select username, account_status, 1 as xs from dba_users
    where account_status != 'LOCKED'
    and username in ('HR', 'SCOTT', 'OUTLN', 'MDSYS', 'CTXSYS');

    exit &exit_status

EOF
```

In this example, *sqlplus* is called and the input is taken from the script until the file marker *EOF* is reached. Output is also redirected to a file in the */tmp* directory. Redirects like this can cause a lot of confusion, but are easily understood if you simply look at it as two separate redirects. One, *<< EOF*, which causes input to be read from the script until the marker *EOF* is reached and another, *> /tmp/audit_locked_accounts_oss.txt,* which redirects the output to the appropriate file. Each redirect acts exactly as it would if the other were not there.

Linking Output to Input with Pipes

Redirecting input and output to files is very powerful and can allow you to process the output of one command with another. UNIX and Linux offer a very powerful shortcut for doing this which will save you the creation of intermediate files.

The *pipe* (|) operator can be placed between two commands to cause the output of the first to be automatically fed to the input of the second. A good example of this is using the *ps* and *grep* commands in conjunction to search for a specific process.

```
$ ps -ef | grep sshd
root      2568      1  0 Oct31 ?        00:00:00 /usr/sbin/sshd
root     30993   2568  0 16:18 ?        00:00:00 sshd: oracle [priv]
oracle   30998  30993  0 16:19 ?        00:00:00 sshd: oracle@pts/1
oracle   31649  30999  0 17:21 pts/1    00:00:00 grep sshd
```

In this example the pipe is used to redirect the rather lengthy output of the *ps -ef* command into the input of the *grep* command. *grep* searches for the pattern *sshd* and prints all lines containing that pattern to the screen.

It is possible to use pipes to connect even more commands together. Here we see the output of the commands from the previous example redirected into the *sort* command.

```
$ ps -ef | grep sshd | sort
oracle   30998  30993  0 16:19 ?        00:00:00 sshd: oracle@pts/1
oracle   31696  30999  0 17:26 pts/1    00:00:00 grep sshd
root      2568      1  0 Oct31 ?        00:00:00 /usr/sbin/sshd
root     30993   2568  0 16:18 ?        00:00:00 sshd: oracle [priv]
```

Through the use of pipes and redirected input and output we will do some fairly sophisticated processing with the basic commands we have covered in this chapter.

Performing Math with expr

One command which does not fit with the others in this chapter is the *expr* command. We will use *expr* later on to perform comparisons and return a true or false answer, but right now let's see how *expr* can be used as a calculator.

expr will take an arithmetic equation as a series of arguments, evaluate it and return the result to the screen or wherever you redirect it. Here is an example to get us started:

```
$ expr 2 + 7
9
```

expr will perform differently on different platforms, but this syntax, including spaces between the numbers and operators of the expression, will work on most platforms. *expr* can be used to perform more than one calculation at once and even respects order of operations.

```
$ expr 4 + 3 \* 3
13
```

The backslash is needed as an escape character to keep the shell from interpreting the asterisk when performing multiplication. This is true with several of the operations which can be performed with *expr*.

When we use *expr* in a shell script, it is likely that instead of numbers we will be using shell variables. We will also often find that we want the result of the expression to be stored in a shell variable. Here is an example of how variables can be used with the *expr* command:

```
$ count=30
$ test=`expr $count \/ 5`
$ echo $test
6
```

Here are some of the more useful operators available for use with *expr*.

OPERATOR	REQUIRES ESCAPE	DESCRIPTION
+	No	Addition
-	No	Subtraction
*	Yes	Multiplication
/	Yes	Division
%	No	Remainder

Table 4.11: *Operators available for use with expr*

Some implementations of the *expr* command support far more advanced functions but simple arithmetic most often will do in our shell scripts.

Conclusion

In this chapter, we have explored many of the building blocks we will use to make our shell scripts. We also introduced the *man* utility to view the online manual pages to find out about commands we have not listed here or learn more about tools that we have.

You will need a text editor to build shell scripts and we covered graphical text editors like you might use on a Windows or Macintosh system. We then went into some depth on the *vi* text editor which is available at the command line. Though difficult to learn, *vi* offers many very powerful features and the advantage of always being available at the command line.

After looking at text editors we saw several other tools which can be used to manipulate text. These tools will mostly be used to do very specific manipulations of text, such as look for a particular pattern or sort it alphabetically.

Process management allows us to control what is happening on the system so we looked at how to view, background, pause, kill and time processes. We also saw how we can make processes keep running with *nohup* in case we loose our connection or log out.

We dug deeper into file and directory permissions. We saw several ways of managing permissions and discussed the affects of certain permission settings.

We explored how we can use files for the input and output of a command. This will allow us to manipulate text files very easily and create logs of what we have done. We also saw how pipes can be used to pass the output from one command to the input of another.

Finally we touched on how the *expr* command can be used to perform simple math. This will allow us to manipulate numbers within our shell scripts and make some more sophisticated analyses.

These are not *all* the tools we will be using in our shell scripts, but they are the most common and some of the most important ones. With a good understanding of what can be done, and this chapter to flip back to for reference, we are ready to start making shell scripts!

Simple Scripting

It has been a long journey to get this far, but we have gained some understanding of many of the individual components which will make up our shell scripts. With a good idea of what the components can do individually and how we can manipulate the input and output between them we should be able to quickly assemble some shell scripts.

Setting Up Your First Script

It is time to start on our first shell script. We will start off with a simple "Hello" style example then build upon it to make it into a script we can use to quickly check some of the vital statistics of the system.

Connect to your system and change to a directory where you can work on your shell scripts. I recommend working in a subdirectory of your home directory called *scripts*. Keeping scripts separate from other files on your system will reduce the possibility that a mistake in a script could destroy or delete something important.

Using *vi* or your text editor of choice create a file named *hello.sh* with the following contents:

🖫 **hello.sh version 1**

```
#!/bin/sh
echo "Hello World!"
```

The first line of this script is special. Known as the *shebang* or *hashbang* this line tells the operating system what program should be used to interpret the contents of this script. In this case, we have specified the Bourne shell executable which, on my system, is found at the path */bin/sh*. To check where the Bourne shell is installed on your system you can type *which sh*.

Before we can execute this shell script we will need to make the file executable with the *chmod* command. For now we will just grant the execute permission to the user who owns this script.

```
$ chmod u+x hello.sh
$ ls -l hello.sh
-rwxr--r--  1 oracle dba 30 Nov 13 17:29 hello.sh
```

Now the script is ready to run. Since we are in the same directory as the script we can use the relative path ./ to run the script.

```
$ ./hello.sh
Hello World!
```

Now we have our first script. While the simple output of "Hello World!" is sufficient to prove that our script is properly set up, it is not a script that you are likely to use very often, so let's make some changes to make it more useful.

Using our text editor we will now replace the word "World" in your script with the variable "$USER" and add a second line to print the hostname.

⌑ hello.sh version 2

```
#!/bin/sh
echo "Hello $USER!"
echo "Welcome to `hostname`"
```

Now if we run hello.sh again we get more output.

```
$ ./hello.sh
Hello oracle!
Welcome to glonk
```

This demonstrates how variables and commands can be used with the *echo* command to provide nicely formatted output. Now we are going to change the name of the script with the *mv* command and make it into a quick system status script.

First use the *mv* command to rename the script to *status.sh*

```
$ mv hello.sh status.sh
```

Now using the editor we will add some lines for common things we might want to check on the system. Disk space, system up time, and load average are probably a good place to start.

status.sh

```
#!/bin/sh
echo "Hello $USER!"
echo "Welcome to `hostname`"
echo "--- Current Disk Usage ---"
df -h
echo "--- Current uptime, users and load averages ---"
uptime
echo "--- Load average numbers represent the 1, 5 and 15 minute load
averages ---"
echo "--- Lower numbers are better for load averages ---"
```

Now when we run the new *status.sh* script we will see not only the output of the *echo* commands, but also the output of the *df* and *uptime* commands executed within the shell script. Here we have used *echo* to provide the user with additional information on the executed commands.

When run we see the output from the *echo* commands right in line with the output from the *df* and *uptime* commands.

```
$ ./status.sh
Hello oracle!
Welcome to glonk
--- Current Disk Usage ---
Filesystem            Size  Used Avail Use% Mounted on
/dev/mapper/VolGroup00-LogVol00
                      72G   6.5G   61G  10% /
/dev/hda1             99M   9.8M   84M  11% /boot
/dev/shm             252M      0  252M   0% /dev/shm
--- Current uptime, users and load averages ---
 19:17:41 up 10 days,  6:02,  2 users,  load average: 0.00, 0.02,
0.00
--- Load average numbers represent the 1, 5 and 15 minute load
averages ---
--- Lower numbers are better for load averages ---
```

Three dashes were used here to make a clear visual separation between the command output and our echoed comments. This is a good way to annotate the output of our shell scripts with or without the dashes.

The Significance of the Shebang

Most of the commands we use have been compiled to run on a system and cannot be easily changed. Rather than being compiled, shell scripts are interpreted. If we run a shell script with the method above, including a shebang and making the script executable, our shell looks at the first line of the script for the shebang and will run the script with the application listed there.

> Shell scripts aren't the only thing to use a shebang to indicate the appropriate interpreter. For example, Perl scripts commonly begin with a shebang followed by the path to the Perl binary.

When the shell script is interpreted by the application, in our scripts the Bourne shell, the line with the shebang is treated as a comment since it starts with a number sign (#). We will explore adding more comments to our script in the next section.

If you exclude the shebang from a shell script you can still use it. To execute it you will need to pass the script name as an argument to the shell binary. This does not guarantee that users will always use the shell you wrote the script for, so it is best to include the shebang.

Unlike the shebang, the *.sh* extension we will use on our shell script names is completely optional. Shell scripts can be named whatever you want them to be, but *.sh* is a common way to indicate shell scripts.

Commenting Your Script

In a shell script, a number sign (#) begins a comment. The number sign and anything following it on the same line is ignored when a script is executed.

I strongly recommend using comments to help others understand what you have done and to make notes for your own future reference. Here are some useful comments I would add to the status.sh script we just viewed.

🖫   **status.sh**

```
#!/bin/sh
#############################################################################
##
# Script Name: status.sh
#
#
#
# Oracle Shell Scripting, Chapter 5
#
#
#
# Usage: status.sh
#
#
#
```

```
# Notes: An example script which shows how information can be echoed to the
#
#        screen to augment command output.
#
#
#
# This script is from the book Oracle Shell Scripting by Jon Emmons
#
# Copyright 2007 Rampant TechPress www.rampant-books.com
#
#
#
# DISCLAIMER: Every environment is different.  This scrip may need to be
#
#             customized before use and any script should be tested in a
#
#             development environment before being used in production.
#
################################################################################
##

# Show the user and host name
echo "Hello $USER!"
echo "Welcome to `hostname`"
echo "--- Current Disk Usage ---"
df -h
# On some systems the -h (human readable) option will not work with df
# In that case you can use the -k option to display output in kilobytes
echo "--- Current uptime, users and load averages ---"
uptime
echo "--- Load average numbers represent the 1, 5 and 15 minute load averages
---"
echo "--- Lower numbers are better for load averages ---"
# These are the first two things I check when I think there is a problem
# with a system, but I'm sure you can think of some other things to add here
```

Near the top of this file we have given some indication of where the script came from and what it does. A line with just a number sign gives a good visual separator to make the comments more readable. Additional comments provide more information on the commands used in the script.

I know what you are thinking. We now have more lines of comments than commands! That's OK. The comments make our script a bit bigger, but even with all these comments the script is still less than 1 kilobyte. The small increase in file size is more than made up for by the improved readability and possible benefits for troubleshooting and further development of the script.

Variables

So far the only variables we have used in our scripts have been ones that are provided automatically by the shell. By introducing our own variables we can customize things even more and even make decisions based on certain values. We will cover that heavily in a later chapter. For now, here are a few examples of how we can set and retrieve variables.

Variables are set using the equal sign (=) with the variable name on the left of the sign and the desired value on the right.

```
$ var1=8
$ text_var='Some text in a variable'
```

Unlike many other languages, in Bourne and bash we do not have to declare the type of data we will put in a variable. Numbers and text can both be put into shell variables. Text containing spaces or special characters can be enclosed in quotes to assign the variable.

To retrieve the contents of a variable we reference the variable name prefixed with a dollar sign ($).

```
$ echo $var1
8
$ echo $text_var
Some text in a variable
```

The *echo* command is a convenient way to view the contents of a variable. We can also add a description to the output.

```
$ echo "Variable var1=$var1"
Variable var1=8
```

Here the variable has been interpreted by the shell and the contents of the variable output. The use of single-quotes will

---

prevent variables from being interpreted, so it is important to use double quotes when working with variables.

A variable can be set to the output of a command by enclosing the command in backtics (`).

```
$ start_time=`date`
$ echo $start_time
Sun Nov 19 17:34:49 EST 2006
```

This provides an easy way to capture the output of a command for further manipulation or future reference.

A variable can be unassigned using the *unset* command. This is not often necessary since variables will automatically be unassigned when the shell script or shell session is completed.

```
$ unset var1
$ echo $var1
```

We also see here that we do not get an error from referencing a variable which is not set. Instead the shell just interprets it as blank.

Variable Scope

When you declare a variable, the variable becomes available from anywhere in the script or session in which you have declared it. The variable and any changes to it will remain in effect until it is cleared using the *unset* command or the script or session ends.

By using the *export* command you can make a variable available to sessions and scripts started by the current session. This will allow us to retrieve the value of the variable from subsequent sessions; however, if the value of the variable is changed in a subsequent session the change will not be reflected in the original shell.

Variable Names

Choosing meaningful and consistent variable names will help keep your scripts readable and make development and troubleshooting easier. While you could use just about anything, I suggest the following conventions:

- Make environmental variables all uppercase

- Make all variables local to a script or session lowercase.

- Use meaningful variable names, even if it means having longer variable names (e.g. use 'start_time' instead of 'st')

- Use underscores to separate words in multi-word variables

- Use only letters, numbers and underscores in variable names

The Bourne and bash shells will not allow you to use variable names which start with numbers or special characters. In addition, special characters like $, #, ! and > cannot be used anywhere in variable names.

Many shell scripts will use short, even one letter variable names. This is generally considered acceptable for loop variables, but should be avoided for other purposes as it makes it difficult to understand the purpose of the variable.

Using Arguments in Your Script

It is very easy to accept arguments into your shell script in the same way arguments are given to other commands. The shell provides a series of variables, *$1*, *$2*, *$3* and so on, that refer to the options, in order, that are given to your script. Another variable, *$@*, represents the complete string of arguments with which the script was called.

> 🔔 The variable $* will also contain the complete list of arguments passed to a script.

To show these variables in action let's consider the following script where we will display the first two arguments and use the *expr* command to find and print their sum:

```
#!/bin/sh
echo "$1+$2=`expr $1 + $2`"
```

Now in a shell session we can put this shell script to work:

```
$ ./add.sh 5 8
5+8=13
```

Arguments can be numbers or character strings. In more complicated scripts we will transfer the arguments to variables with more meaningful names, but for now this example is enough to show how arguments work.

Another variable, *$#* will contain the number of arguments passed to a script. This can be useful when checking to see that an expected number of arguments was given.

Prompting for Input

Another way to assign values into variables is by prompting for input from the user. By taking information interactively you can write scripts which will require input, but the user does not need to know ahead of time what arguments are required. You may even have a script which asks for different information based on other conditions in the system.

By using the *read* command we can read a single line of input from the standard input, which is typically a user at a keyboard. The content of that line is then put in the variable specified.

```
#!/bin/sh
echo "Enter your name"
read name
echo "Hi $name.  I hope you like this script"
```

In this script we use *echo* to tell the user what we expect them to enter and then *read* to put the input into the variable *name*.

```
$ ./welcome.sh
Enter your name
Jon
Hi Jon.  I hope you like this script
```

Read can also be used to grab multiple values into separate variables, or even to read a single line from a text file. In some scripts we will even see how we can use *read* to prompt for input only if arguments are not supplied.

Debugging Shell Scripts

Sooner or later (probably sooner) you will run a script and it will not do what you expected it to. There are lots of steps you can take to try to figure out what is wrong. Here are some of the ones I use most often.

Place Temporary Markers in the Script

When you are not sure if a script is running a certain block of code, simply add a line that will output a marker to the screen. Simple lines like *echo "Before First if statement"* or *echo "Within First else"* can help you quickly determine which blocks of code are being executed and which are not. Do not be afraid to put several of these in a script during development. Just make sure you take them out before the script goes into production or better yet comment them in case you need them for later development.

```
echo "At line 23"
```

Echo Variables to the Display

Much of the behavior of our shell scripts will be dependant on the values in variables. Often simply echoing the variables to the screen will help you determine why a certain behavior is happening.

The *env* command can be used to display all environmental variables which are variables that have been exported, e.g. ORACLE_SID. There are typically quite a few of these but they can help you quickly determine the environmental variables set at a certain point in time.

If you wish to check on specific script variables you can use the *echo* command to print them to the screen. It is often useful to add a little text so you will know which variable you are looking at.

```
echo "count=$count"
```

Starting the Script in Debug Mode

The Bourne and bash shells have provided some very useful resources for debugging shell scripts. The *-v* option will print each line of the shell script including comments to the standard output before it is executed. To enable the *-v* option we can add it to the end of the shebang line. That will cause the shell to be invoked with the -v option.

Here is the output of the status.sh script with the -v option added to the shebang:

```
$ ./status.sh
#!/bin/sh -v
#
```

```
# status.sh script by Jon Emmons
# Published in Oracle Shell Scripting, Rampant TechPress, 2007
#
# A simple script to provide some information about the system
# Show the user and host name
echo "Hello $USER!"
Hello oracle!
echo "Welcome to `hostname`"
hostname
Welcome to glonk
echo "--- Current Disk Usage ---"
--- Current Disk Usage ---
df -h
Filesystem            Size  Used Avail Use% Mounted on
/dev/mapper/VolGroup00-LogVol00
                       72G  6.6G   61G  10% /
/dev/hda1              99M  9.8M   84M  11% /boot
/dev/shm             252M     0  252M   0% /dev/shm
# On some systems the -h (human readable) option will not work with
df
# In that case you can use the -k option to display output in
killobytes
echo "--- Current uptime, users and load averages ---"
--- Current uptime, users and load averages ---
uptime
 21:34:55 up 16 days,  8:20,  1 user,  load average: 0.00, 0.00,
0.00
echo "--- Load average numbers represent the 1, 5 and 15 minute load
averages ---"
--- Load average numbers represent the 1, 5 and 15 minute load
averages ---
echo "--- Lower numbers are better for load averages ---"
--- Lower numbers are better for load averages ---
# These are the first two things I check when I think there is a
problem
# with a system, but I'm sure you can think of some other things to
add here
```

With the -v option we get a lot of output, but this can be invaluable when trying to find the cause of an error.

The *-x* option provides a different output of the commands executed. Each command is displayed before it is executed but *after* variables have been substituted for their values. To make the commands stand out from the output each line showing the command begins with a plus (+) symbol. Here is the output of our status.sh script with the -x option.

```
$ ./status.sh
+ echo 'Hello oracle!'
```

```
Hello oracle!
++ hostname
+ echo 'Welcome to glonk'
Welcome to glonk
+ echo '--- Current Disk Usage ---'
--- Current Disk Usage ---
+ df -h
Filesystem            Size  Used Avail Use% Mounted on
/dev/mapper/VolGroup00-LogVol00
                       72G  6.6G   61G  10% /
/dev/hda1              99M  9.8M   84M  11% /boot
/dev/shm             252M     0  252M   0% /dev/shm
+ echo '--- Current uptime, users and load averages ---'
--- Current uptime, users and load averages ---
+ uptime
 22:08:16 up 16 days,  8:53,  1 user,  load average: 0.07, 0.02,
0.00
+ echo '--- Load average numbers represent the 1, 5 and 15 minute
load averages ---'
--- Load average numbers represent the 1, 5 and 15 minute load
averages ---
+ echo '--- Lower numbers are better for load averages ---'
--- Lower numbers are better for load averages ---
```

With the *-x* option, commands which are executed as part of another command, like the *hostname* command which is executed within the second *echo* command, are shown with an additional plus before them.

These two options can be combined to provide a very verbose debugging output showing each command line before and after variable substitution. Here is a partial listing of the status.sh script with the *-vx* option.

```
$ ./status.sh
#!/bin/sh -vx
#
# status.sh script by Jon Emons
# Published in Oracle Shell Scripting, Rampant TechPress, 2007
#
# A simple script to provide some information about the system
# Show the user and host name
echo "Hello $USER!"
+ echo 'Hello oracle!'
Hello oracle!
echo "Welcome to `hostname`"
hostname
++ hostname
+ echo 'Welcome to glonk'
Welcome to glonk
...
```

The combination of these two options can provide useful debugging information but with a very large script may be overwhelming. When the extended output is desired it may be easiest to send the output to a text file. Since the debugging output is sent to *standard error* output it can easily be redirected to a file with *2>debug.txt* after the command similar to what we saw in the last chapter.

In general, you will not want to use either of these options unless you have a problem. The amount of output they generate can cause confusion, but if you are stuck trying to understand a problem, these options can shed some light on what the system is seeing and running.

Conclusion

We have finally seen our first shell script. The examples in this chapter were simple, but simple is good. If you can create a "Hello World" program and then make a script with some more complicated output you are well on your way.

We now know when a script is made executable with the *chmod* command the *shebang* is interpreted by the shell to determine what program should be used to execute the script. This is key to making our scripts run like other programs.

Comments can make our shell scripts more readable for other developers and for our own future reference. Using meaningful variable names is also very important to making our scripts easy to work with.

We saw how arguments can be used with our script as a way to take input. If we want a more interactive script we can also use the *read* command to take input directly from the keyboard.

Important debugging options, *-v* and *-x* were covered and how they can provide additional useful output for tracking down problems. These options, separately or together, can speed troubleshooting considerably.

So by now you should be comfortable writing a quick script to run a few commands and get some output. That may not seem like much, but if you start to incorporate more of the commands from chapter 2 you can see how you can write a script to check disk space, check some log files, confirm that a process is running, and much more. Things will get more sophisticated from here, but not all shell scripts need to be complicated. Often the most useful ones are the simple ones.

Interacting with SQL*Plus

The main way we interact with an Oracle database from the UNIX command line is with Oracle's SQL*Plus. SQL*Plus offers not only the ability to interface with the data in our database but, since version 8i, also offers the ability to configure and control the database.

Since SQL*Plus is so good at interacting with the database, there are countless benefits to being able to control it with our shell scripts.

Calling SQL Scripts from Shell Scripts

If we want to start SQL*Plus just to run a SQL script we can very easily give the script name as an argument to the *sqlplus* command. We can even include the username and password right on the command line.

For this example we will use the following *database_status.sql* script.

🖫 database_status.sql

```
set pagesize 0 linesize 80 feedback off

SELECT 'The database ' || instance_name ||
' has been running since ' || to_char(startup_time, 'HH24:MI
MM/DD/YYYY')
FROM v$instance;

SELECT 'There are ' || count(status) ||
' data files with a status of ' || status
```

```
FROM dba_data_files
GROUP BY status
ORDER BY status;

SELECT 'The total storage used by the data files is ' ||
sum(bytes)/1024/1024 || ' MB'
FROM dba_data_files;

SELECT 'There are ' || count(*) ||
' control files'
FROM v$controlfile;

SELECT 'Online archive log group ' || group# || ' contains ' ||
count(thread#) || ' thread(s)'
FROM v$log
GROUP BY group#
ORDER BY group#;

SELECT 'The archive log mode is ' || log_mode ||
' and the archiver is ' || archiver
FROM v$database, v$instance;

exit;
```

We could enter *sqlplus*, login, and run this script with the @ symbol, but instead we specify the username, password, and script name at the command line. Here is the *sqlplus* command in the context of a shell script.

database_status.sh

```
#!/bin/sh
sqlplus -S system/manager @database_status.sql
```

With this method we should make sure the .sql script and the .sh script are both in the working directory when we execute them. If we do that we can execute this script and see the results:

```
$ ./database_status.sh
The database oss has been running since 14:20 12/02/2006
There are 5 data files with a status of AVAILABLE
The total storage used by the data files is 955 MB
There are 3 control files
Online archive log group 1 contains 1 thread(s)
Online archive log group 2 contains 1 thread(s)
Online archive log group 3 contains 1 thread(s)
The archive log mode is NOARCHIVELOG and the archiver is STOPPED
```

The *-S* option for *sqlplus* suppresses the information that *sqlplus* normally prints to the screen on startup making our query results the only thing to be printed.

> Having the username and password entered on the command line may expose them to other users viewing running processes (those using the *ps* command.) We will see later in this chapter how to avoid this problem.

This should give you some ideas of how *sqlplus* can be easily controlled by a shell script to give output from the database. Using a shell script to call an SQL script in this way introduces the complexity of creating, versioning and moving multiple files for a single task.

This method can be useful if working with a provided shell script, especially those provided by Oracle. When calling Oracle provided scripts from the ORACLE_HOME directory, a shortcut can be used. A question mark (?) used in the path of a script will be expanded to be the Oracle home directory allowing you to refer to scripts in the Oracle home directory without specifying the full path.

```
$ sqlplus "/ as sysdba" @?rdbms/admin/utlrp.sql
```

The argument given above describes the location of the *utlrp.sql* script within the Oracle home directory. In the next section, we will see how we could include our SQL right in the shell script. That will give us the advantage of having only one script instead of two.

Embedding SQL within a Shell Script

Typically when we start SQL*Plus from the command line it will expect a user at a keyboard to enter commands. By using an

---

input redirect, signified by a double less-than sign (<<), the shell will send SQL*Plus input from our shell script rather than having it wait for user input. This eliminates the need for a user entering commands or a *.sql* file.

In the last section we used two scripts, a .sql script and a .sh script to call *sqlplus* to execute. To make *sqlplus* read commands from our script we use the double less-than sign and give it a marker which will be matched with an identical marker at the end of the SQL commands. This example should help make things more clear.

```
#!/bin/sh
sqlplus -S system/manager << EOF
set pagesize 0 linesize 80 feedback off

SELECT 'The database ' || instance_name ||
' has been running since ' || to_char(startup_time, 'HH24:MI
MM/DD/YYYY')
FROM v\$instance;

SELECT 'There are ' || count(status) ||
' data files with a status of ' || status
FROM dba_data_files
GROUP BY status
ORDER BY status;

SELECT 'The total storage used by the data files is ' ||
sum(bytes)/1024/1024 || ' MB'
FROM dba_data_files;

SELECT 'There are ' || count(*) ||
' control files'
FROM v\$controlfile;

SELECT 'Online archive log group ' || group# || ' contains ' ||
count(thread#) || ' thread(s)'
FROM v\$log
GROUP BY group#
ORDER BY group#;

SELECT 'The archive log mode is ' || log_mode ||
' and the archiver is ' || archiver
FROM v\$database, v\$instance;

exit;
EOF
```

This shows the *<< EOF* in place of the SQL script. Notice the *EOF* at the end of the script which indicates the end of the commands for *sqlplus*. Other shell commands could appear after this EOF marker.

EOF is commonly used as a marker to stand for 'end of file'. In actuality any word could be used as a marker as long as it is unique within this script. When this method is used more than once in a script it is common to use EOA, EOB, EOC, and so on to represent separate input sections. These words do not have to be all uppercase either. This is simply a convention to make them easier to locate within the script.

In the script above, we select from several 'v$' tables within Oracle. Since the dollar sign indicates a variable within the shell we need to escape it with a backslash before the dollar sign (\$) to cause the shell not to interpret the variable. In other scripts we will use shell variables within the SQL by omitting the escape character.

Prompting for a password

In the example we have been using so far we have explicitly stated the password 'manager' in the script. Of course it is advisable to change your passwords on a regular basis and never to use the default passwords.

If we leave the password in the shell script like this we would need to update our shell script every time we change our system password. That would be fine for one shell script, but when you have a dozen or a hundred shell scripts on different systems and databases this quickly becomes cumbersome. One option for avoiding this problem is to prompt the user for a password.

```
#!/bin/sh
echo "Enter the system password for $ORACLE_SID"
```

```
read system_pw
sqlplus -S system/$system_pw << EOF
set pagesize 0 linesize 80 feedback off

SELECT 'The database ' || instance_name ||
' has been running since ' || to_char(startup_time, 'HH24:MI
MM/DD/YYYY')
FROM v\$instance;

SELECT 'There are ' || count(status) ||
' data files with a status of ' || status
FROM dba_data_files
GROUP BY status
ORDER BY status;

SELECT 'The total storage used by the data files is ' ||
sum(bytes)/1024/1024 || ' MB'
FROM dba_data_files;

SELECT 'There are ' || count(*) ||
' control files'
FROM v\$controlfile;

SELECT 'Online archive log group ' || group# || ' contains ' ||
count(thread#) || ' thread(s)'
FROM v\$log
GROUP BY group#
ORDER BY group#;

SELECT 'The archive log mode is ' || log_mode ||
' and the archiver is ' || archiver
FROM v\$database, v\$instance;

exit;
EOF
```

By using the method we saw in chapter 4 of prompting for input, the user will now be able to enter the password for this database when the script is run. While this may seem redundant since Oracle would prompt for the password if none were provided, this is a handy method if you need to enter *sqlplus* multiple times in the same script.

```
$ ./db_status.sh
Enter the system password for oss
manager
The database oss has been running since 14:20 12/02/2006
There are 5 data files with a status of AVAILABLE
The total storage used by the data files is 955 MB
There are 3 control files
Online archive log group 1 contains 1 thread(s)
Online archive log group 2 contains 1 thread(s)
```

```
Online archive log group 3 contains 1 thread(s)
The archive log mode is NOARCHIVELOG and the archiver is STOPPED
```

This method also increases security in two ways. First, the password is not listed in a file on the system eliminating the possibility of a user stumbling on your shell script and finding out your system password. Second this keeps the password from showing up in *ps* listings with the *sqlplus* command. The biggest drawback to this method is that when you enter the password when prompted it is displayed on the screen. This is also unsuitable for scripts which run automatically since a user will not be there to enter a password.

Reading a Password from a File

Another way to avoid the perils of having passwords in your shell scripts is to store database passwords in a text file. When using this method, special attention needs to be paid to the permissions on the text password files. The method for securing important files discussed in chapter 4 will generally be sufficient.

We can easily adapt our example above to read a password from a file, but first we will need to create the text file with the password. This could be created anywhere, but since it applies to a specific database, I suggest keeping it within the admin directory for that database. For the purposes of demonstration, I will create a *passwords* directory within the admin directory. You may want to choose a less obvious name for your passwords directory.

Here is how I set up my passwords directory. I have removed all permissions on the directory for everyone but the user who owns it.

```
$ cd /u01/app/oracle/admin/oss
$ mkdir passwords
$ chmod g-rwx,o-rwx system.pw
```

```
$ ls -ld passwords
drwx------   2 oracle dba 4096 Dec  3 14:59 passwords
$ cd passwords
$ echo 'manager' > system.pw
$ chmod g-rwx,o-rwx system.pw
$ ls -l system.pw
-rw-------   1 oracle dba 8 Dec  3 15:06 system.pw
```

By redirecting output from the *echo* command we can easily create our password file without the need for an editor. The result is a text file which contains only the word *manager*. Again, we remove the group and other permissions so no one but the oracle user can view this file. The *.pw* extension here is simply a convention. You could use any extension here or no extension at all. I do strongly recommend using the user's name as part of the file name as it will make it easy to discern multiple password files from one another.

Now that we have the password file set up and secured we can update our script to use it as input. We will use the *cat* command to read the contents of the file and the equal sign to assign it to our system_pw variable.

```
#!/bin/sh
system_pw=`cat /u01/app/oracle/admin/oss/passwords/system.pw`
sqlplus -S system/$system_pw << EOF
set pagesize 0 linesize 80 feedback off

SELECT 'The database ' || instance_name ||
' has been running since ' || to_char(startup_time, 'HH24:MI
MM/DD/YYYY')
FROM v\$instance;

...
```

The second line is the important one so I have excluded the end of the script to save trees. Using this method we both avoid having the password hard-coded in the script and having to prompt the user for it each time the script is run. We also will not expose the password in the *ps* listing. This is ideal for scripts which will be run automatically by the system.

Running shell commands from SQL*Plus

Under certain circumstances we will want to run a shell command without exiting *sqlplus*. The exclamation point allows us to temporarily suspend our SQL session and execute a shell command.

If we want to add some system information to our db_status.sh script we just need to put the appropriate shell commands right in line with our SQL commands.

```
#!/bin/sh
system_pw=`cat /u01/app/oracle/admin/oss/passwords/system.pw`
sqlplus -S system/$system_pw << EOF
set pagesize 0 linesize 80 feedback off

SELECT 'The database ' || instance_name ||
' has been running since ' || to_char(startup_time, 'HH24:MI
MM/DD/YYYY')
FROM v\$instance;

!echo "Hostname is `hostname` and the platform is `uname`"

SELECT 'There are ' || count(status) ||
' data files with a status of ' || status
FROM dba_data_files
GROUP BY status
ORDER BY status;

...
```

In this case we are checking on the hostname and platform of the system. When we run this script the shell command is executed and its output printed inline with the SQL output.

```
$ ./db_status.sh
The database oss has been running since 15:48 12/03/2006
Hostname is localhost.localdomain and the platform is Linux

There are 5 data files with a status of AVAILABLE
The total storage used by the data files is 955 MB
There are 3 control files
Online archive log group 1 contains 1 thread(s)
Online archive log group 2 contains 1 thread(s)
Online archive log group 3 contains 1 thread(s)
The archive log mode is NOARCHIVELOG and the archiver is STOPPED
```

The exclamation point tells *sqlplus* that we want to open a shell session and execute a command. This has the same effect as the *host* command in *sqlplus* but I prefer the exclamation point for its relative terseness.

Instead of using the exclamation point within our SQL we could exit *sqlplus*, execute commands on the command line and re-enter *sqlplus* to continue running SQL commands. This would work but would take more time and system resources as *sqlplus* would need to be launched more than once.

Passing variables into SQL*Plus

While Oracle provides some powerful ways to get data into a database sometimes we will want to pass things directly from our shell scripts. There are a couple methods we can use for this.

SQL Script Arguments

Just like our shell scripts can have arguments, we can also have arguments for our SQL scripts. These are also known as *script parameters*. The script parameters are given after the *@scriptname.sql* either within *sqlplus* or when *sqlplus* is initiated.

The script arguments will be set in the SQL session as substitution variables named 1, 2, 3 and so on. They can be referenced with an ampersand. Consider this SQL script:

```
select 'Selecting everything from the table &1' from dual;
select * from &1;
exit;
```

By passing a table name when we call the script we can use this script to select from a specific table:

```
$ sqlplus system/manager @select_table.sql 'v$instance'

SQL*Plus: Release 10.2.0.1.0 - Production on Mon Dec 4 23:12:38 2006

Copyright (c) 1982, 2005, Oracle.  All rights reserved.


Connected to:
Oracle Database 10g Enterprise Edition Release 10.2.0.1.0 -
Production
With the Partitioning, OLAP and Data Mining options

old   1: select 'Selecting everything from the table &1' from dual
new   1: select 'Selecting everything from the table v$instance'
from dual

'SELECTINGEVERYTHINGFROMTHETABLEV$INSTANCE'
---------------------------------------------
Selecting everything from the table v$instance

old   1: select * from &1
new   1: select * from v$instance

INSTANCE_NUMBER INSTANCE_NAME
--------------- ----------------
HOST_NAME
----------------------------------------------------------------
VERSION           STARTUP_T STATUS        PAR    THREAD# ARCHIVE
LOG_SWITCH_WAIT
----------------- --------- ------------ --- ---------- ------- ----
-----------
LOGINS     SHU DATABASE_STATUS   INSTANCE_ROLE      ACTIVE_ST BLO
---------- --- ---------------- ------------------ --------- ---
              1 oss
localhost.localdomain
10.2.0.1.0        03-DEC-06 OPEN         NO          1 STOPPED
ALLOWED    NO  ACTIVE            PRIMARY_INSTANCE   NORMAL    NO


Disconnected from Oracle Database 10g Enterprise Edition Release
10.2.0.1.0 - Production
With the Partitioning, OLAP and Data Mining options
```

Since these are substitution variables, Oracle will place the values into the statement before the SQL is parsed. While substitution variables are less efficient than bind variables in some circumstances they can be used to specify parts of the sql statement like column or table names while bind variables can only be used for values.

Multiple arguments can be specified after the script name and arguments that contain spaces must be enclosed in quotes. In the example above, the table name *v$instance* is enclosed in single quotes to keep the shell from interpreting the dollar sign as the beginning of a variable.

Shell Variables and Embedded SQL

Earlier in this chapter we saw how SQL can be embedded in a shell script. One side benefit to this method is that we can use shell variables to represent values within the embedded SQL. In the following *user_info.sh* script, we pass a username to the script as an argument. It is transferred to a variable named lookup for better readability and the variable lookup is used in the WHERE clause within the SQL.

```
#!/bin/sh
lookup=$1
sqlplus -S system/manager << EOF
SELECT username, account_status, expiry_date
FROM dba_users WHERE lower(username)=lower('$lookup');
exit;
EOF
```

The result is a single script which can take an argument and execute SQL using the value of that argument. This can be a very efficient way to load data into Oracle tables without the need for a load file or other intermediate step.

Getting Information Out of SQL*Plus

The familiar *spool* SQL command is one of the primary ways we will get data out of our database, but there are a couple other options we should keep in mind.

First, as presented in chapter 4, we can redirect *standard output* or *standard error* with the greater than (>) sign. This allows us to place SQL output into files which can be manipulated by our shell script. When using this method, it is handy to use the *-S* option for *sqlplus* to suppress the application info that is normally printed at startup. This helps minimize the unnecessary information written to the file.

The second method we can use to send information back to the shell is the exit status. The exit status acts as an indicator of the success of a command. When we exit *sqlplus* we can set an exit status of 0, indicating success, or another integer, indicating some type of failure.

The example below is from the *audit_locked_accounts.sh* script which we will see in chapter 12. It demonstrates both the redirect of output and the setting of an exit status.

```
tempfile=/tmp/audit_locked_accounts_$ORACLE_SID.txt

# Start sqlplus and check for locked accounts
sqlplus -S "/ as sysdba" << EOF > $tempfile

    set pagesize

    select 'The following accounts were found to be unlocked and
should not be'
    from dual;

    define exit_status = 0

    column xs new_value exit_status

    select username, account_status, 1 as xs from dba_users
    where account_status != 'LOCKED'
    and username in ('HR', 'SCOTT', 'OUTLN', 'MDSYS', 'CTXSYS');

    exit &exit_status

EOF

# If the exit status of sqlplus was not 0 then we will send an email
if [ $? != 0 ]
then
    mail -s "Accounts Unlocked in $ORACLE_SID" oracle < $tempfile
fi
```

The *$tempfile* variable in this script is set to the location of the temporary file this script will use. It is important to note here that the output is redirected into the file which the variable describes and not into the contents of the variable.

The SQL in this script manipulates the exit status by providing a variable, which has already been set to 0 or 1, as an argument to the *exit* command. Exit status will be covered in more detail in chapter 8.

Conclusion

At this point you should have a good idea of how we can control SQL*Plus through our shell scripts. SQL*Plus will be our main window into the database, so it is important to be able to get exactly what we want into and out of it.

Calling SQL scripts with the at sign (@) and the script name as an argument to the *sqlplus* is a simple and familiar way to run SQL from our shell scripts. This method is particularly applicable when we are using some type of prefabricated SQL scripts such as those provided by Oracle. This way we can call the SQL without having to modify vendor provided scripts.

Embedding SQL in our shell scripts simplifies things in a different way. By using this method for our custom SQL, we can create shell scripts which employ *sqlplus* but which do not need a separate SQL file to function.

Whichever method we use we will inevitably need passwords to connect to the database. Though simple, placing the password in plain text as an argument to the *sqlplus* command poses a security risk so we discussed how passwords can be either prompted for or read from a password file and placed in a shell variable. The shell variable can then safely be used in place of the password when calling *sqlplus*.

But shell scripting and *sqlplus* is not a one-way street. We also saw how we can use the exclamation point to run commands in a shell session without exiting our SQL session.

Finally we discussed a few methods for moving data between *sqlplus* and the shell. Later on we will be using these methods to load and extract data and make sophisticated decisions based on the values we pass around.

In the next chapter we will cover some of the methods that can be used to make decisions at the command line.

Making Decisions

Shell scripts that show us some values or run a complex command are handy, but much more becomes possible when we can make some decisions. Decisions may be based on the time of day, how busy a resource is, or who is executing the script.

Eventually we will have scripts which automatically make adjustments, for instance restarting the listener if it is unavailable. While much of this logic could be written within PL/SQL code I prefer to do this work at the shell and keep the SQL simple. After all, this is a shell scripting book not a PL/SQL book.

Conditional Expressions

In our scripts we will use *conditional expressions* to decide whether to execute a block of code or not. The conditional expression may be comparing two strings of text, checking to see if a file is readable, or comparing the contents of variables. Conditional expressions always evaluate to true or false which is represented by 0 and 1 respectively.

It may seem unusual to have 0 represent true, but there is a good reason for it. Every command in UNIX and Linux actually returns a hidden result code called an *exit condition* which represents the success or failure of that command. Since there are several reasons a command may fail but really only one way it can succeed we interpret the result code of zero to be success and anything else to represent failure. This allows commands to use a proprietary integer to represent different means of failure which may then be interpreted by other commands or by the user. We will cover more about how to view the exit condition in chapter 8.

For the most part we can regard the results of a conditional expression as *true* or *false* and not have to worry about this 0 and 1 stuff for now. Conditional expressions will be used within the context of an *if* statement or a loop and its evaluation will determine the code to be executed.

Everything makes more sense with examples, so here is an example of how we can use conditional expressions as part of an *if* statement at the command line.

```
$ age=29
$ if [ $age -lt 30 ]
> then
> echo "You're still under 30"
> fi
You're still under 30
```

We will go into more detail on the *if* statement in the next section, for now let's talk about the conditional expression. In most applications we will enclose the conditional expression in square brackets as seen above. This example compares the contents of the variable $age, that we have set to 29, with the number 30. *-lt* indicates that the shell should check to see if $age is *less than* 30. Similarly *-gt* would be greater than and *-eq* would be equal. There are several more comparisons which can be done within an expression. Some of the most commonly used ones are listed in the tables below.

Everything between the brackets must evaluate to true or false. Once evaluated, if true, the shell will execute the text between the *then* and the *fi* keywords. If the expression evaluated to false, the shell would skip the code after the *then* keyword and continue with the next command after the *fi*.

Comparing Numbers

There are several useful mathematical comparisons which can be made within conditional expressions. Here are some of the most commonly used:

COMPARATOR	MATHEMATIC EQUIVALENT	EVALUATES TO TRUE IF
-eq or =	=	the values on each side of the comparator are equal
-ne or !=	≠	the two values are not equal
-gt	>	the first value is greater than the second
-ge	≥	the first value is greater than or equal to the second
-lt	<	the first value is less than the second
-le	≤	the first value is less than or equal to the second

Table 7.1: *Mathematical Comparators*

Any of these comparators can be used to compare two numbers, whether expressed as integers or the contents of variables. If you try to compare text with these comparators you will receive an error, with the exception of = and !=, that will be examined next, the shell will provide you an often useless error.

Comparing Text

Numbers are not all we can compare. We might want to know if one string matches another or if there is any information in a string. When comparing strings we can either use variables which contain strings of text or use strings of text in either single or double quotes.

```
$ if [ $ORACLE_SID = "oss" ]
> then
> echo "Using the sid for the Oracle Shell Scripting database"
> fi
Using the sid for the Oracle Shell Scripting database
```

Here we have checked to see if the contents of the ORACLE_SID environmental variable match the string "oss." Since it does, the code in the *then* section of the statement is executed. Here are some of the other things we can check for with strings.

COMPARATOR	EVALUATES TO TRUE IF
=	the string on each side of the comparator are identical
!=	the string on each side of the comparator are not identical
string	the length of the string is not zero

Table 7.2: *String Comparators*

string is listed here to represent a variable name. If the variable is set to something other than a null string the condition will be evaluated to true. Here is a common example to see if the $ORACLE_SID variable is set.

```
$ if [ $ORACLE_SID ]
> then
> echo "ORACLE_SID variable is set to $ORACLE_SID"
> fi
ORACLE_SID variable is set to oss
```

Later on we will use a decision like this to determine if we need to set some Oracle related variables and possibly run the *oraenv* command.

Checking Files

There are also several things we can check about files. We can check to see if a file exists, compare the last time the files were modified, or check the permissions on a file.

COMPARATOR	EVALUATES TO TRUE IF
-nt	the file listed before is newer than the file listed after the comparator

-ot	the file listed before is older than the file listed after the comparator
-e	the file exists
-d	the file is a directory
-h	the file is a symbolic link
-s	the file is not empty (has a size greater than zero)
-r	the file is readable
-w	the file is writable

Table 7.3: *File Comparators*

The first two comparators listed above are used to compare two files to each other. All the other file comparators in this list simply check a specific condition of the file and will only expect a file to be listed after the comparator. Here's an example of when we might want to check for the existence of a file.

```
$ if [ -e $ORACLE_HOME/dbs/init$ORACLE_SID.ora ]
> then
> echo "An init file exists for the database $ORACLE_SID"
> fi
An init file exists for the database oss
```

Since many of our shell scripts will be dependant on other files for both input and output, it will often be prudent to check that the necessary files exist and are readable or writeable as we start our script. This will give us the opportunity to abort the script if the required files are not available as well as the chance to give meaningful feedback to the user.

Combining Comparisons

We can combine multiple comparisons into a single expression in order to perform more complicated checks. The ultimate result of a complex expression will still be either *true* or *false* but by combining expressions we can check for several things at once.

```
$ if [ -e $ORACLE_HOME/dbs/init$ORACLE_SID.ora -a -e \
> $ORACLE_HOME/dbs/spfile$ORACLE_SID.ora ];
```

```
$ then
$ echo "We seem to have both an spfile and an init file"
$ fi
We seem to have both an spfile and an init file
```

The *-a* comparator in the statement above acts as a logical *and* causing the entire condition to evaluate to *true* if, and only if the expression on each side of the *-a* evaluates to *true*. Similarly *-o* could be used as an *or* causing the expression to evaluate to true if either the first condition, the second condition, or both evaluate to true.

One final option for modifying comparators is the exclamation mark (!) which can be used to negate any expression. This allows us to check if a condition is *false*.

```
$ if [ ! -e $ORACLE_HOME/dbs/orapw$ORACLE_SID ]
> then
> echo "There's no password file in the default location for this
database"
> fi
There's no password file in the default location for this database
```

This negation can be used in combination with *and* and *or* to form some fairly sophisticated logic.

COMPARATOR	EVALUATES TO TRUE IF
-a	the expressions on each side of the comparator are both true
-o	one or both of the expressions are true
!	The following expression is false

Table 7.4: *Comparator Modifiers*

There are methods to combine these comparators in even more complicated ways, but we will see later in this chapter that these complex comparisons are often better made with nested *if* statements. This will help keep our scripts more readable as well as give us more flexibility on what we can do with the results.

Making Simple Decisions with if and else

Conditional expressions allow us to ask a question about variables, files, or our environment. Once we have the answer to a question, the *if* statement is the simplest way we can go about acting on it.

In the last section we used several *if* statements to demonstrate some simple conditional expressions. This is the simplest form of the *if* statement where we say "*If* this condition is true, *then* execute this code." The end of an *if* statement is indicated by the *fi* keyword, simply *if* spelled backwards.

```
$ age=29
$ if [ $age -lt 30 ]
> then
> echo "You're still under 30"
> fi
```

In order to make it more clear where the *if* statement begins and ends we will indent everything between the *if* and the *fi*. We will also further indent the commands between the *then* and the next keyword to show where the execution of that specific part of the *if* completes. While unnecessary, these two conventions become invaluable when dealing with complex scripts.

Within the context of a script the example above should look like this:

```
#!/bin/sh
age=29
if [ $age -lt 30 ]
    then
            echo "You're still under 30"
fi
```

Some prefer to indent with tabs while others prefer to use a series of spaces. The scripts included with this book are indented with tabs. Since most text editors allow you to control where you would like your tabs to stop I find this method more flexible.

Anyway, back to the *if* statement. If the condition given is found to be true, based on the rules presented in the last section, the code after the *then* keyword will be executed until it comes upon either an *fi*, indicating the end of the *if* statement, an *else* keyword, which will be covered next, or an *elif*, which will be covered later in this section. When the *if* statement has hit one of these keywords the rest of the shell script will be executed starting directly after the *fi*.

Quite often we will want to perform one task if a condition is true, but another different task if it is false. Within an *if* statement commands following the keyword *else* are executed when the conditional statement is evaluated to *false*.

```
#!/bin/sh
age=29
if [ $age -lt 30 ]
    then
            echo "You're still under 30"
    else
            echo "You're 30 or over"
fi
```

This code will now execute the first *echo* command if the variable age is less than 30, but if that turns out to be false the second *echo* command will be executed. Each *if* statement must have a *then* clause, the *else* is optional. Upon the execution of the *if* statement, either the *then* or *else,* if present, code will be executed, but never both.

Hopefully you can start to see how the indenting is important to keeping our scripts readable. It does make the scripts marginally bigger, but does not affect execution and will make troubleshooting scripts considerably easier.

Secondary Checks with elif

Another option within an *if* statement is an *elif* or else-if clause. If the initial condition of the *if* statement is evaluated to be *false,* a second condition can be tested with an *elif.* A conditional expression following an *elif* is evaluated in the same way as with an *if* but it is important to remember that it will only be evaluated if the *if* statement fails.

```
#!/bin/sh
age=39
if [ $age -lt 30 ]
    then
            echo "You're still under 30"
    elif [ $age -ge 30 -a $age -le 40 ]
            then
                    echo "You're in your 30s"
    else
            echo "You're 40 or over"
fi
```

In this example we set the age variable to 39. Upon execution, the condition after the *if* statement is found to be false so the code after the *then* would not be executed. It would proceed to evaluate the expression after the first *elif* statement which evaluates to true, therefore the code after the *then* following the first *elif* would be executed. After that the shell would continue after the *fi* statement.

You may have noticed that in the last paragraph I referred to the *first elif.* Within an *if* statement there may be multiple *elif* statements each with their own conditional expression. The shell will execute each one in order until the first one succeeds. After the first one succeeds it will exit the *if* statement and continue executing after the *fi.* If neither the *if* nor any *elif* conditional statements evaluate to *true,* the code following the *else* will be executed, if present.

```
#!/bin/sh
age=49
```

```
if [ $age -lt 30 ]
      then
              echo "You're still under 30"
      elif [ $age -ge 30 -a $age -le 40 ]
            then
                    echo "You're in your 30s"
      elif [ $age -ge 40 -a $age -le 50 ]
            then
                    echo "You're in your 40s"
      else
              echo "You're 50 or over"
fi
```

By using a series of *elif* statements we can cover several potential execution paths in a single statement; however, there is another option we can use when we want to compare text. In the next section we will talk about the *case* statement.

Choosing from a list with case

The *case* offers a way to decide between several options more simply than a series of *if then elseif else* statements. While the *case* statement is limited to comparing strings it can be very powerful for that.

```
#!/bin/sh
case $ORACLE_SID
in
    oss)
            echo "Using the sid for the Oracle Shell Scripting
database"
            ;;
    db1)
            echo "Using the default Oracle database"
            ;;
    *)
            echo "I don't have a description for this database"
            ;;
esac
```

This script shows the use of a *case* statement to carry out a specific action if the ORACLE_SID variable matches the value *oss* or *db1*, but has a separate action for any other value for ORACLE_SID.

A *case* statement will be followed by the variable we would like to compare followed by the *in* keyword. Then one possible pattern is provided (in quotes if it contains whitespace characters) followed by a close parentheses. The code to be executed is given, and the option is terminated by two semicolons. The final option above is an optional catch-all which will be executed if no other pattern is matched.

A * is not the only expression which can be used here. In most implementations, *case* will take most of the regular expression syntax. When executed, the patterns are compared in order and only the commands following the first statement are executed. Because of this you should be careful what order your options are in and put the more broad catch-all ones, especially *, toward the end of the list.

The example above could be rewritten with an *if* statement as below, but the different options are far less clear. To debug this statement you would have to look at each conditional statement.

```
#!/bin/sh
if [ $ORACLE_SID="oss" ]
    then
            echo "Using the sid for the Oracle Shell Scripting
database"
    elif [ $ORACLE_SID="db1" ]
            then
                    echo "Using the default Oracle database"
    else
            echo "I don't have a description for this database"
fi
```

If we want to be a little less specific on our ORACLE_SID case above we can use a simple regular expression to accept any number in a SID that starts with 'db'.

```
#!/bin/sh
case $ORACLE_SID
in
    oss)
```

```
              echo "Using the sid for the Oracle Shell Scripting
database"
              ;;
    db[0-9])
              echo "Using something like the default Oracle database"
              ;;
    *)
              echo "I don't have a description for this database"
              ;;
esac
```

This simple modification allows us to avoid having a separate case for 'db1', 'db2', 'db3', and so on. Using regular expressions like this helps keep our code succinct and readable.

These statements allow us to choose if we want to execute one piece of code or another, but sometimes we want to execute some commands multiple times. That is where loops come in.

The while Loop

The *while* loop behaves similar to the simple *if* statement in that it will check a condition and execute some commands if the condition is true. Unlike the *if* command, when it is done executing the code it is given it then checks the condition again. If the condition is still true it will execute the same code again.

The *while* loop will continue doing this until the given condition is found to be false, then it will skip the given code and the script is continued after the *done* keyword.

```
#!/bin/sh
i=1
while [ $i -le 10 ]
do
    echo "The current value of i is $i"
    i=`expr $i + 1`
done
```

This simple example shows the variable *i* being set initially to 1. The *while* loop checks the conditional statement and notices that *i* is in fact less than or equal to 10 so it executes the code between the *do* and *done* keywords. The second line sets *i* to the result of *i* + *1* using the *expr* command. This is a typical way to increment the loop counter within a loop.

> 💣 It is important to make sure that something is modifying the loop counter and that it will eventually cause the *while* condition to fail. Otherwise you will end up in an infinite loop! If this happens, refer to the Managing Processes section in Chapter 4.

After the first execution of the *while* loop the variable *i* now contains 2. The conditional statement is evaluated again and, since it is still true, the commands are executed again. This goes on until *i* is equal to 11. At that point the conditional expression fails, the commands are not executed and the script will continue on after the *done* keyword.

> 🔔 We have talked about using meaningful identifiers, but *i* probably does not seem very meaningful! It is not, but it is typical for single letter variables to be used as counters in loops. This is acceptable when the variable has no use other than a loop counter.

When executed the output of the script above will look like this:

```
$ ./while.sh
The current value of i is 1
The current value of i is 2
The current value of i is 3
The current value of i is 4
The current value of i is 5
The current value of i is 6
The current value of i is 7
The current value of i is 8
The current value of i is 9
The current value of i is 10
```

We do not always have to compare a variable to a static number like 10. We could instead prompt the user and read a number into a variable, then use that variable to set the limit for executions of the loop. The counter does not always have to go up by 1 either. Any expression could be used to modify the counter and there may be times where you want your counter to increase by more than one each time through the loop or even count backwards.

We will see more of the *while* loop as we get into the scripts. We will even see some examples that check for a file and stop executing only if the file is missing! This will allow us to have a crude means to cause a process to stop when we do not have interactive control over it.

The for Loop

The *for* loop offers us the ability to repeat the same commands a certain number of times based on a list of values. The commands between the *do* and *done* keywords after a *for* statement are repeated once for each item in a list of values. The *for* loop even places the list item it is currently processing in a variable for us to use within the loop.

```
#!/bin/sh
count=0
for i in 2 4 6
do  ·
    echo "i is $i"
    count=`expr $count + 1`
done
echo "The loop was executed $count times"
```

In this example, we have provided *2 4 6* as separate values to the *for* loop. The loop will be executed once for each of these values and will set the value of *i* to the value for which it is currently executing so we can use the *i* variable within the loop. Within this we also added a secondary *count* variable to count and report the number of times this loop executes.

```
$ ./for.sh
i is 2
i is 4
i is 6
The loop was executed 3 times
```

For loops are not just for numbers. Later we will use a list of ORACLE_SIDs to perform the same action on several databases. We can even provide a variable which contains a list of values.

```
#!/bin/sh
files=`ls`
count=0
for i in $files
do
     count=`expr $count + 1`
done
echo "There are $count files in the current directory"
```

Here we have taken a listing of the current directory and used a *for* loop to parse over each file. We are not doing anything with the files here, but instead are just adding 1 to *count* for each file. This shows how we can easily parse over a list within a variable.

Breaking Out of Loops

Sometimes in a loop we need to deal with the unexpected and get out of a loop before another evaluation is completed. To do that, we can use a *break* statement. The *break* will cause the shell to stop executing the current loop and continue on after the end of that loop.

```
#!/bin/sh
files=`ls`
count=0
for i in $files
do
     count=`expr $count + 1`
```

```
    if [ $count -gt 100 ]
    then
            echo "There are more than 100 files in the current
directory"
            break
    fi
done
```

break can be called anywhere between the *do* and *done* of a loop. We may want to break if a certain keyword is read or if a value exceeds a threshold. Above, we break out of the *for* loop if the variable *count* exceeds 100. After the *break* keyword the shell will skip forward and continue after the *done* for the *for* loop.

Next we will cover *nested loops*, loops within loops. When using nested loops the *break* command will only exit the inner most loop unless given a number as an argument. If a number is given it will break out of that number of loops starting with the innermost loop.

Nesting Loops

Loops within loops are common in any programming but they can become confusing very quickly! Diligence with keeping your commands well organized and properly indented will help immensely when you start creating nested loops.

With this script, we are using a *for* loop to parse over each argument passed into the script. Within that we have a loop which will multiply the number passed in with each number from 1 to 10.

```
#!/bin/sh
for num in $*
do
    echo "Multiplication table for the number $num"
    i=1
    while [ $i -le 10 ]
    do
            echo "$num x $i = `expr $num \* $i`"
            i=`expr $i + 1`
```

```
      done
done
```

Upon execution quite a few things are going to happen, but if we take a look at the output below everything makes sense.

```
$ ./multi_table.sh 2 7
Multiplication table for the number 2
2 x 1 = 2
2 x 2 = 4
2 x 3 = 6
2 x 4 = 8
2 x 5 = 10
2 x 6 = 12
2 x 7 = 14
2 x 8 = 16
2 x 9 = 18
2 x 10 = 20
Multiplication table for the number 7
7 x 1 = 7
7 x 2 = 14
7 x 3 = 21
7 x 4 = 28
7 x 5 = 35
7 x 6 = 42
7 x 7 = 49
7 x 8 = 56
7 x 9 = 63
7 x 10 = 70
```

On the first time through the *for* loop the variable *num* is set to 2. The *while* loop then executes with i set to 1 through 10, each time through printing the equation of *num* multiplied by i. Once that is done the *for* loop repeats the entire process with *num* set to 7.

 Be careful about reusing variable names in nested loops! *i* is fine as a counter for one loop, but if you have another loop inside that loop with a counter called *i* you're going to have some unexpected results.

Eventually we will be using loops inside of *if* statements inside of other loops and so-on. As long as you keep your indenting consistent and watch your variable names you should not have too much trouble.

Conclusion

Conditional expressions, decisions and loops are what really make shell scripting powerful. The ability to make predictable decisions based on variables and to repeat commands will allow us to make the machine do many times more work than we could alone.

Conditional expressions are at the core of all loops and decisions. With them we can check to see if a value is what it should be, make sure we are within a reasonable number, or even check on file attributes. These checks can be combined into complex conditions allowing us to check on more than one thing at a time.

The basic decision statement we will use is the *if* statement. It will allow us to check a condition and execute certain code if the statement is true. Optionally we could have a second check with an *elif* statement or an *else* statement with code which is only executed if the *if* and *elif* statements have failed.

The *case* statement gives us a way to name a list of possibilities which will then be compared with a variable. Only the code after the first matching possibility will be executed making for an easy decision when we want more than a *true/false* option.

for and *while* loops will allow us to repeat commands for a set of values. *for* loops take a list of values, but *while* loops are more open-ended, simply checking a condition before each execution.

Things can start getting difficult when we start nesting loops but this allows us to work through many different options with very little programming.

We will be using many of these methods to check for prerequisites, input, output, success, and errors in the next chapter.

Checking and Reporting Results

When working with databases and systems we are constantly concerned with the results of our work. If a command has a syntax error, we want to know about it eventually, if a backup fails, we want to know about it soon, if a database is down we probably want to know about it immediately!

In this chapter we will examine how we can poll the system, databases, and even the output from our own scripts to look for possible problems. It is not enough just to identify problems, so we will also see some different methods we can use to handle or make a human aware of the problem. Effectively checking for and reporting problems will help us be able to respond to issues often before they affect users.

The Exit Status: The Unseen Result

Whenever a command is run in UNIX or Linux it will complete with a status of either success or failure. We often see the indication of a failure in the form an error message to the screen. What we typically do not see is the commands *exit status*.

The exit status of the command is set as the shell variable *?*. If the command is successful the ? variable will be set to 0. If the command fails ? will be set to some other integer value, often 1.

The value of ? can be viewed in the same way other shell variables are with the *echo* command.

```
$ ls
error.txt      log1.log  log3.log  myfile.txt  sample.txt
types_of_unix.txt
listing.txt  log2.log  marx.txt  output.txt  test_script.sh
$ echo $?
0
$ ls *.dmp
ls: *.dmp: No such file or directory
$ echo $?
1
$
```

Though 1 is often used to indicate failure a command may set the value of ? to something other than 1 to indicate a specific type of failure. For instance, 127 is often used to indicate a 'command not found' error. This can be very useful for error reporting and debugging but is specific to each command. Refer to the man page for a specific command to learn more about its possible exit statuses.

Despite there being several possible values to indicate failure, the point that there is only one to indicate success makes it very easy to programmatically determine and respond to a command's success or failure with an *if* statement.

In this script, we will use *tail* to look at the last 42 lines of the alert log for the current instance. If the command fails for some reason we want to give some feedback on why it may have failed so we have used an *if* statement to echo some output if the exit status of the command is *not* zero.

```
#!/bin/sh
#
# Script to show the last 48 lines of the alert log for the
# current Oracle SID.
# Requires ORACLE_BASE and ORACLE_SID be set
# Assumes OFA file layout
#
tail -42 $ORACLE_BASE/admin/$ORACLE_SID/bdump/alert_$ORACLE_SID.log
if [ $? != 0 ]
then
        echo "Something went wrong.  Look for errors in this output
and"
```

```
        echo "check that the TAIL command is in your path, that the
alert"
        echo "log is in the appropriate OFA location and that the
ORACLE_BASE"
        echo "and ORACLE_SID variables are set"
fi
```

We will see a lot of this type of checking in the scripts included with this book. Sometimes we recognize a failure and report it, others we will perform a different action or even exit the script when a command fails.

Setting the Exit Status of a Shell Script

Like commands, scripts will provide an exit status when they complete. By default, a script will exit with the status of the last command executed in the script. That means if the last command was successful the script would give an exit status of 0. If the last command failed the script will give a non-zero exit status.

If desired, it is easy to override the default behavior of shell scripts and provide a customized exit status. Simply provide the exit status number as an argument to the *exit* command in your shell script.

```
exit 99
```

The exit status could be used to indicate a particular condition to other scripts which may be calling this one. The exit status can be any integer from 0 to 255, but it is best to use the convention of 0 for success and 127 for command not found. You could use exit status 1 to indicate a failure or another integer, other than 0 and 127, as a custom failure message.

Setting the Exit Status for SQL*Plus

Like other commands, sqlplus will set the exit status variable when it completes. Unlike most other commands, sqlplus gives us the ability to set the exit status upon exiting!

Under normal circumstances when we type the exit command within sqlplus, the exit status will be set to 0. If there is a login failure sqlplus will fail and set the exit status to 1. There are a few ways we can set the exit status to something other than 0 or 1.

When calling the exit command from within sqlplus, we can manually set the exit status by providing a value as an argument.

```
SQL> exit 12
Disconnected from Oracle Database 10g Enterprise Edition Release
10.2.0.1.0 - Production
With the Partitioning, OLAP and Data Mining options
$ echo $?
12
```

If used within a PL/SQL block we could use this to indicate the success or failure of a prior command or the result of a certain check within the database.

We can also tell sqlplus to automatically exit with a certain status when it encounters as SQL error. Doing this will cause sqlplus to exit without completing the current script and set the exit status to the indicated value.

```
SQL> whenever sqlerror exit 99
SQL> select * from notable;
select * from notable
              *
ERROR at line 1:
ORA-00942: table or view does not exist


Disconnected from Oracle Database 10g Enterprise Edition Release
10.2.0.1.0 - Production
With the Partitioning, OLAP and Data Mining options
$ echo $?
99
```

This can be a convenient catch-all for handling SQL errors within scripts. Within the shell script we would simply add an if statement to examine the variable ? and notify us that there was an SQL error if the value is set to 99.

The number 99 was chosen here as an arbitrary value. You can use any value from 0 to 255 but if you wish to indicate a custom failure code it is best to avoid 0, 1 and 127 which indicate success, failure and command not found respectively.

Scanning Logs for Output

If you are the database administrator you already know that it is important to check certain log files on a regular basis. This may be one of the most useful things we can put in a shell script.

Typically we will want to know almost immediately when there is an ORA- error in any of our production databases. We can easily use the *grep* command to check our logs and notify us if the pattern ORA- is found.

```
#!/bin/sh
#
# Script to check the alert log for ORA- errors
# Requires ORACLE_BASE and ORACLE_SID be set
# Assumes OFA file layout
#
alert_log=$ORACLE_BASE/admin/$ORACLE_SID/bdump/alert_$ORACLE_SID.log
grep ORA- $alert_log > /dev/null
if [ $? = 0 ]
then
        echo "The following ORA- errors were found in $alert_log"
        grep ORA- $alert_log
fi
```

This script checks the alert log for the string 'ORA-' with the *grep* command. By redirecting the output of this first grep command to /dev/null we prevent the lines from being printed at this time. Instead, we use the exit status of the grep command to determine if lines were found. If no matching lines are found, grep would set the exit status to 1 indicating a failure. If one or more matches are found, *grep* exits with a status of 0 indicating success.

We then examine the value of $? with an if statement. If we find it is zero we know that *grep* found ORA- errors in the log. At that point we print a custom message indicating that errors were found and then re-execute the grep command, this time allowing the results to be printed to the standard output.

In chapter 11 we will see how the output of a script like this can be put in an email and automatically sent to the administrator. With email and scheduling via cron, this script can be made to check the alert log on a regular basis and notify the administrator when there is a problem. Similar scripts can be used to check other logs on the system.

Later in this book we will see how we can easily send email from a script. This will allow us to be notified of results from scripts which are run automatically.

Checking the Output of Commands

Sometimes the exit status of a command does not tell us enough. It is fairly easy to manipulate commands with simple output but complicated output will require more processing.

Command output is often manipulated with a combination of *grep*, *sed*, *awk*, *cut* and other text manipulation commands. Those who do a lot of text manipulation may find that they can accomplish complex text manipulation with only tools like *sed* and *awk*. For the casual scripter it is often easier to combine several tools each of which performs a small portion of the processing.

```
up=`uptime`

# Parse out the current load averages from the uptime command
load_1=`echo $up | awk -F "load average: " '{ print $2 }' | cut -d,
-f1 | cut -d. -f1`

load_5=`echo $up | awk -F "load average: " '{ print $2 }' | cut -d,
-f2 | cut -d. -f1`

load_15=`echo $up | awk -F "load average: " '{ print $2 }' | cut -d,
-f3 | cut -d. -f1`
```

The code segment above first takes the result of the *uptime* command and puts it into the variable *up*. This is what the output looks like before processing:

```
$ uptime
 18:08:52 up 24 days,  9:10,  4 users,  load average: 3.87, 37.95,
31.29
```

The *uptime* output is parsed in several steps and the result is stored in a variable. To get the 1 minute load average, the first one listed, the echo command is used to print the *uptime* output to the standard output. *awk* is then used to print the second column while treating the string "load average: " as a field separator. This is an effective way to print everything that follows a certain string.

After this initial processing we are left with the following output:

```
3.87, 37.95, 31.29
```

From here the *cut* command is used to hone in on the exact load average we are looking for. The *-d* option allows us to specify the use of a comma as a separator and the *-f* option lets us specify which field we want to retrieve. Here the *cut* command is used to perform a function very similar to what we did with *awk*; however, *cut* can only be used with a single character delimiter but *awk* can use a multi-character string.

Checking the Output of Commands

165

After the *cut -d -f1* the output has been cut down to just the number 3.87. Another *cut* command is used to eliminate the decimal point and everything after it. This leaves us with just the number 3 which would then be placed in the variable *load_1*.

All this processing allows us to take a mixed text/number output and carve it down to a single integer so we can process it within the shell. If you want to see how this fits into the entire script take a look at monitor_load_average.sh in chapter 16.

Conclusion

The exit condition of a command is very useful for determining its success or failure. Though somewhat counterintuitive having 0 indicate success and 1 indicate failure makes it trivial to use these values programmatically.

By default, a shell script will have the exit status of the last command run. If you want to override its exit status you can give a number as an argument to the *exit* command.

Like other commands, SQL*Plus sets an exit status when it completes. Even more useful is that we can manipulate the exit status and use it to indicate a condition in the database even though the SQL*Plus command has run successfully.

We also used the *grep* command to scan the alert log for errors. This method is very common for scanning logs for specific output and can reduce the need to manually check the log for errors.

Command output can be passed through commands to find specific information. We saw how tools like *awk*, *grep* and *cut* can be used together to get exactly what we want even from complex output.

We will use the exit condition in a slightly different way in the next chapter. We'll also see how multiple commands and scripts can be run in order, simultaneously, or conditionally based upon the success or failure of the previous command.

Making the Shell Behave

While the focus of this book is to use shell scripts to combine shell commands, there are a few shortcuts we can use to quickly tie together commands and scripts. These methods can be used within shell scripts, but are more often used at the command line to achieve basic flow control.

Listing multiple commands on one line

If we want to simply execute a command at the command prompt, and then execute another immediately after the first completes, we can easily accomplish this by separating the two commands with a semicolon (;). This is particularly useful if the first commands are expected to take a long period of time and we do not want to wait around just to start the second command.

A good example of this is with a database export. If we want to take a full export then compress the export file with the gzip utility we could run the *exp* command, wait the minutes to hours it may take to complete, then execute the gzip command to compress the file. Instead we can put both commands on the same command line.

```
$ exp USERID=system/manager FULL=y FILE=export.dmp; gzip export.dmp

Export: Release 10.2.0.1.0 - Production on Thu Jan 18 18:20:00 2007

Copyright (c) 1982, 2005, Oracle.  All rights reserved.


Connected to: Oracle Database 10g Enterprise Edition Release
10.2.0.1.0 - Production
```

```
With the Partitioning, OLAP and Data Mining options
Export done in US7ASCII character set and AL16UTF16 NCHAR character
set
server uses WE8ISO8859P1 character set (possible charset conversion)

About to export the entire database ...
. exporting tablespace definitions
. exporting profiles
. exporting user definitions
...
```

Placing a semicolon after the first command tells the shell to execute that command as if it were the only thing on the line. The shell then continues and executes the command after the semicolon. It is possible to put more than two commands on the same command line using this method, but if you get much more than three or four you should consider putting them into a small shell script instead.

> When listing multiple commands on each line like this and if a command is cancelled or fails for some reason, subsequent commands are still executed. Because of this you should avoid using this method in cases where the success of a command may affect what you want to do next.

Another way to execute multiple commands on the same line is by separating them with ampersands (&). When a list of commands is given separated by ampersands each job is started immediately in the background.

```
$ dbstart & lsnrctl start &
[1] 11921
[2] 11922
$
LSNRCTL for Linux: Version 10.2.0.1.0 - Production on 18-JAN-2007
18:39:26

Copyright (c) 1991, 2005, Oracle.  All rights reserved.
```

Just like when an individual command is started in the background, the shell reports the job number and process

---

number. They can then be viewed and controlled with the *jobs*, *fg* and *bg* commands.

When using this method it will be difficult to tell what command output is coming from since it is all written to the standard output. Nonetheless, if you are not concerned with the output of the commands, this is a quick way to kick off several commands at once.

Conditional Execution

The methods described above allow us to execute multiple commands with no regard for the outcome of previous commands. When we want to make the execution of a command conditional on the success or failure of a previous command we use a slightly different method.

Let's say we want to create an export of the database then compress it. In the first example in this chapter we did exactly that, but regardless of the outcome of the export the shell would then try to compress a file called export.dat. Instead we can use a double ampersand (&&) between the commands to indicate that the second command should be run if, and only if, the first command is successful.

```
$ exp USERID=system/manager FULL=y FILE=export.dmp && gzip
export.dmp

Export: Release 10.2.0.1.0 - Production on Thu Jan 18 19:03:03 2007

Copyright (c) 1982, 2005, Oracle.  All rights reserved.


Connected to: Oracle Database 10g Enterprise Edition Release
10.2.0.1.0 - Production
With the Partitioning, OLAP and Data Mining options
Export done in US7ASCII character set and AL16UTF16 NCHAR character
set
server uses WE8ISO8859P1 character set (possible charset conversion)

About to export the entire database ...
```

```
. exporting tablespace definitions
. exporting profiles
...
```

Now if the *exp* command fails for some reason, we do not waste any time compressing a possibly corrupt export. The exact same results could be achieved with an *if* statement within a shell script, however, though less flexible the double-ampersand is much more succinct.

In other situations we may want to execute a command only when a previous command has failed for some reason. In this case we can use a double-pipe (||).

```
$ exp USERID=system/manager FULL=y FILE=export.dmp || mail_me.sh

Export: Release 10.2.0.1.0 - Production on Thu Jan 18 19:03:03 2007

Copyright (c) 1982, 2005, Oracle.  All rights reserved.


Connected to: Oracle Database 10g Enterprise Edition Release
10.2.0.1.0 - Production
With the Partitioning, OLAP and Data Mining options
Export done in US7ASCII character set and AL16UTF16 NCHAR character
set
server uses WE8ISO8859P1 character set (possible charset conversion)

About to export the entire database ...
. exporting tablespace definitions
. exporting profiles
...
```

In this example, the *exp* command is run and if the export command fails, the mail_me.sh script will be executed. The *mailme.sh* script shown here simply sends an email to a given address that something needs attention. We will look at this script in chapter 11.

Listing Long Commands on Multiple Lines

When a command or set of commands is too long to fit on one line, the shell will typically wrap the text onto the next line, even if the break happens in the middle of a word. To avoid this, a backslash (\) can be used to allow a command to be continued on the next line.

```
$ exp USERID=system/manager FULL=y FILE=export.dmp \
> && gzip export.dmp

Export: Release 10.2.0.1.0 - Production on Thu Jan 18 19:28:52 2007

Copyright (c) 1982, 2005, Oracle.  All rights reserved.


Connected to: Oracle Database 10g Enterprise Edition Release
10.2.0.1.0 - Production
With the Partitioning, OLAP and Data Mining options
Export done in US7ASCII character set and AL16UTF16 NCHAR character
set
server uses WE8ISO8859P1 character set (possible charset conversion)

About to export the entire database ...
. exporting tablespace definitions
. exporting profiles
```

By following the exp command with a backslash we can then type enter and complete this statement on the next line. Notice that the prompt changes to a greater than symbol to indicate that we are continuing the same command. We could then add a backslash on the next line to continue onto a third. When there is a line without a backslash on it, the shell will interpret the entire command as if it were all typed on one line.

We will also see this method used within shell scripts. Commands with lots of arguments (like *exp*) or long path names are more easily displayed when spread out over multiple lines.

Using the methods presented here it is possible to chain together a very long string of commands, but we should be careful not to consider these shortcuts a substitute for shell scripting. When a script is going to be running unattended or sophisticated logic or feedback is required, a shell script is probably preferable.

Backslash as an Escape Character

When we use a backslash to continue a command on the next line we are actually telling the shell to ignore the enter character that immediately follows it. Normally when the shell sees an enter character it executes what is on the command line, but the backslash prevents the shell from interpreting it. We can also use a backslash to keep the shell from interpreting other special characters.

There are several characters which get special treatment in the shell. A few examples are the space, & and $ characters. When we want to use these characters literally rather than having the shell interpret them, we can add a backslash before the special character.

```
$ echo You should be paying your DBA more \$
You should be paying your DBA more $
```

> It is generally considered bad practice to use special characters in a file name, but once in a while someone does. To manipulate these files you can simply precede each special character with a backslash. For example a file named "my text file.txt" could be referenced at the command line as "my\ text\ file.txt".

If there are multiple special characters you need to escape, you can escape them each individually with backslashes, but another option is to use single quotes.

Single Quotes

Single quotes can be used around text to prevent the shell from interpreting any special characters. Dollar signs, spaces, ampersands, asterisks and other special characters are all ignored when enclosed within single quotes.

```
$ echo 'All sorts of things are ignored in single quotes, like $ & *
;  |.'
All sorts of things are ignored in single quotes, like $ & * ; |.
```

When handling strings of text this is a very efficient way to prevent the shell from interpreting special characters or trying to substitute variables. Even semicolons are ignored when placed between single quotes.

Since the newline character is not interpreted between single quotes, a string within single quotes can easily be made to span multiple lines.

```
$ echo 'Text within single quotes can
> span multiple lines
> because the newline character
> is not interpereted'
Text within single quotes can
span multiple lines
because the newline character
is not interpereted
```

The only thing you can not put within single quotes is a single quote. Fortunately we have another type of quote we can use.

Double Quotes

Double quotes act similar to single quotes, except double quotes still allow the shell to interpret dollar signs, back quotes and backslashes. We already know that backslashes prevent a single special character from being interpreted. This can be useful within double quotes if we need to use a dollar sign as text instead of as a variable. It also allows us to escape double quotes so they will not be interpreted as the end of a quoted string.

```
$ echo "Here's how we can use single ' and double \" quotes within
double quotes"
Here's how we can use single ' and double " quotes within double
quotes
```

You may have also noticed that the apostrophe, which would otherwise be interpreted as the beginning of a quoted string, is ignored within double quotes. Variables, however, are interpreted and substituted with their values within double quotes.

```
$ echo "The current Oracle SID is $ORACLE_SID"
The current Oracle SID is oss
```

Like single quotes, text within double quotes can span multiple lines. Though double quotes are more flexible in what they display, there are times then the use of single quotes can be used to eliminate the need for escape characters which can make a script easier to understand.

Back Quotes

Back quotes are wholly unlike single or double quotes. Instead of being used to prevent the interpretation of special characters, back quotes actually force the execution of the commands they enclose. After the enclosed commands are executed their output is substituted in place of the back quotes in the original line. This will be clearer with an example.

```
$ today=`date '+%A, %B %d, %Y'`
$ echo $today
Friday, January 19, 2007
```

Here we have set the value of the variable *today* to the output of the *date* command. The shell will execute the command *date '+%A, %B %d, %Y'* which will print the day, date and year as output. The shell then places that output in place of the back quoted string and sets the value of the variable *today*.

A command within back quotes can be used nearly anywhere in the shell. These will be evaluated and substituted before the rest of the line is executed.

Exit a Shell Script Anytime

There may be certain conditions on which you want to exit a script without executing the rest of the commands. This is commonly used when a script checks for prerequisites and one or more of the prerequisites fails.

🖫 check_alert_log.sh (partial listing)

```
#!/bin/bash

# Add /usr/local/bin to the PATH variable so the oraenv command can
be found
PATH=$PATH:/usr/local/bin; export PATH

# If a SID is provided as an argument it will be set and oraenv run
# otherwise we will use the current SID.  If no SID is set or
provided
# an error message is displayed and the script exits with a status
of 1
if [ $1 ]
then
    ORACLE_SID=$1
    ORAENV_ASK=NO
    . oraenv
else
    if [ ! $ORACLE_SID ]
    then
        echo "Error: No ORACLE_SID set or provided as an
argument"
        exit 1
    fi
fi
...
```

The code above shows how the *exit* command is used within a set of *if* statements. The first *if* statement checks for an argument being passed to the script. If there is no argument the *else* block of the statement will be executed. Within the *else* another *if* statement checks the variable ORACLE_SID. If the variable was *not* set, an error is displayed and the *exit* command is used to stop the execution of this script.

As seen in the script excerpt above, the *exit* command can accept an argument. The argument can be a number from 0 to 255 and will set the *exit status* of the shell script for other commands to interpret.

Conclusion

This chapter has introduced some different ways to control the shells behavior. Though sometimes difficult to understand, these techniques are invaluable when trying to get a shell command or script to behave exactly the way you want.

We saw how the semicolon can allow us to execute several commands in sequence. This can keep us from having to wait around for one command to finish just to execute the next.

Conditional execution allows us to execute multiple commands with a little more intelligence. By using && and || we can easily have the outcome of a command determine if subsequent commands will be executed.

Through the use of backslashes we can take long commands and spread them over multiple lines. This is useful when executing long commands or if the shell prompt is very long. The backslash can also be used as an escape character to prevent special characters from being interpreted by the shell.

Another method of controlling what the shell interprets is through the use of single and double quotes. Single quotes inhibit all special characters from being interpreted and instead treats them like plain text. Double quotes allow a few characters ($, \ and `) to be interpreted but inhibits all others.

We also saw how back quotes can be used to execute a command or string of commands and substitute their output into the original line. Finally the exit command was shown as a way to stop the execution of a script at any point.

In the next chapter we will see how we can automate tasks to happen without our intervention. This can help liberate the administrator from many routine tasks.

Making Scripts Run Automatically

Shell scripting allows us to take a long and complex series of commands and combine them into an easy to run script. When you have tasks that need to be run on a regular basis, the next step is to automate them completely.

In this chapter we will discuss how we can make scripts run on a regular schedule, when we log in or out of a system, or even at system startup or shutdown. With some well written scripts it is possible to make a database nearly maintenance free.

Scheduling Repeating Tasks with Cron

The cron Daemon

The cron *daemon* is the system task that runs scripted jobs on a pre-determined schedule. The crontab command is used to tell the cron daemon what jobs the user wants to run and when to run those jobs.

Each user on the system may have their own *crontab file* unless they have been restricted by the system administrator. The crontab file is only manipulated using the *crontab* command and should never be edited directly.

crontab Command Options

The *crontab* command allows us to view, edit, or replace the current user's crontab file. If you receive an error like the

---

following when you run the *crontab* command, you will need to ask your system administrator to allow you to setup a crontab.

```
$ crontab -e
crontab: you are not authorized to use cron.  Sorry.
```

This table shows the common options for the *crontab* command. Notice that only the root user can change other user's crontabs.

OPTION	PURPOSE
-e	edit the current *crontab* file using the text editor specified by the *EDITOR* environment variable or the *VISUAL* environment variable
-l	list the current *crontab* file
-r	remove the current *crontab* file
-u	specifies the user's *crontab* to be manipulated. This is usually used by *root* to manipulate the *crontab* of other users or can be used by you to correctly identify the *crontab* to be manipulated if you have used the *su* command to assume another identity.

Table 10.1: *crontab options*

To list the current user's crontab, you can use the *-l* option for the *crontab* command.

```
$ crontab -l
# Daily full export
00 01 * * *     /u01/app/oracle/admin/oss/scripts/full_export.sh
# Weekly full hot backup
00 03 * * 0     /u01/app/oracle/admin/common/scripts/hot_backup.sh
oss 0
# Nightly incremental hot backup
00 03 * * 1-6   /u01/app/oracle/admin/common/scripts/hot_backup.sh
oss 1
```

By using the *-e* option for the crontab command we can edit the current user's crontab. This will bring a copy of the crontab up in your default editor. You can then edit the crontab and when you exit the editor the crontab command will put your changes in place.

crontab also accepts a file name and will use the specified file to create the crontab file. Many users prefer to use this option rather than the crontab -e command because it provides a master file from which the crontab is built, thus providing a backup to the crontab. The following example specifies a file called mycron.tab to be used as the input for crontab.

```
$ crontab mycron.tab
```

To delete the current user's crontab you can use the -r option. This will remove all jobs from the crontab.

```
$ crontab -r
```

The Format of the crontab File

The crontab *file* consists of a series of entries specifying what shell scripts to run and when to run them. It is also possible to document crontab entries with comments. Lines that have a pound sign (#) as the first non-blank character are considered comments. Blank lines are completely ignored. Comments cannot be specified on the same line as cron command lines but rather must be kept on their own lines within the crontab.

crontab Entries

Each *crontab* entry line is comprised of six positional fields specifying the time, date, and shell script or command to be run. The format of a crontab entry is described in the table below:

Field	Minute	Hour	Day of Month	Month	Day of Week	Command
Valid values	0-59	0-23	1-31	1-12	0-6	Command path/command

Each of these fields can contain a single number, a range of numbers indicated with a hyphen (such as *2-4*), a list of specific values separated by commas (like *2,3,4*), or a combination of these designations separated by commas (such as *1,3-5*). Any of these fields may also contain an asterisk (*) indicating every possible value of this field. This can all get rather confusing so let's take a look at a few examples.

```
# Daily full export
00 01 * * *    /u01/app/oracle/admin/oss/scripts/full_export.sh
```

This entry will run the *full_export.sh* script at 0 minutes past 1 am, every day of the month, every month of the year, and every day of the week. As with our shell scripts, comments help make the crontab file more readable.

```
# Weekly full hot backup
00 03 * * 0    /u01/app/oracle/admin/common/scripts/hot_backup.sh
oss 0
```

This entry runs at 3:00 am, but only on Sundays (day 0.) While the day of month and month fields have asterisks this entry will only be run on Sundays since crontab entries will only be executed when all the given values are met.

```
# Nightly incremental hot backup
00 03 * * 1-6   /u01/app/oracle/admin/common/scripts/hot_backup.sh
oss 1
```

In this entry we have specified that the script should be run at 3:00 am Monday through Saturday.

```
00,15,30,45 * * * *
/u01/app/oracle/admin/common/scripts/check_disk_space.sh
```

This entry has minutes separated by a comma indicating that it should be run at each of the indicated times. Since all the other fields are wildcards (*) the entry will be run on the hour (00), 15 minutes past the hour, 30 minutes past the hour and 45 minutes past the hour for every hour of the day and every day of the year.

```
00 12 * * 1-5 /home/oracle/lunch_time.sh
```

This lunch reminder is set up to run at 12:00 p.m. Monday through Friday only.

The most important thing to remember is that a crontab entry will execute every time all of its conditions are met. To take the last entry as an example, any time it is 00 minutes past the hour of 12 on any day of the month and any month of the year and the day of the week is between Monday and Friday inclusive (1-5) this crontab will be executed.

You will use wildcards in most crontab entries but be careful where you use them. For instance, if we mistakenly placed a * in the minute position of the last crontab example above we would end up running the script for *every* minute of the 12:00 hour instead of just once at the beginning of the hour. I do not think anyone needs that many reminders to go to lunch, do you?

We have explored how to specify the date and time in the crontab but what about the command? Well, most folks will write shell scripts to execute with their crontab entries but you can actually just execute a command from the crontab as well. Either way, be sure you put the absolute path to your command in the crontab.

If the command or script you call in your crontab sends output to the screen, some systems will attempt to email the output to the owner of the crontab file. This can be useful, but where is that email going? If you are checking the account regularly or forwarding the email to another account this may be sufficient, but as we will see in the next chapter it can be much better to create a custom email within the script and handle any output that way.

Another option is to redirect that output to a log file with the >> symbol so you can check it later. Be careful with this as the log files may get rather large over time!

Scheduling One-Time Tasks with at

We have seen how *cron* can be used to schedule repeating tasks, but it is not unusual to have a task which needs to be run once, but at a time when we do not want to run it manually. For these tasks we can use the *at* command to schedule the job.

The *at* command is used to schedule tasks for execution at a certain date and time. The syntax for *at* is surprisingly simple! The *at* command takes the time you wish to run the commands at as an argument. If you are running a command later in the same day you do not have to specify any more than that.

```
$ at 23:30
at> /u01/app/oracle/admin/oss/scripts/full_export.sh
at> ctrl-d <EOT>
job 5 at 2007-01-21 23:30
```

After entering *at* and the desired time of execution, the *at* command allows you to enter the commands or scripts that you wish to run. You can enter one or many commands here and when you are done type control-d. *at* then prints the job number and date which it will be run.

at can also take a date on which to run the command. The date is given in MMDDYY format, but the word *tomorrow* can also be used instead of a numeric date. Here we have also added the *-m* option to send mail to the user upon completion of this *at* job.

```
$ at -m 11:00 tomorrow
```

```
at> /u01/app/oracle/admin/oss/scripts/full_export.sh
at> ctrl-d <EOT>
job 6 at 2007-01-22 11:00
```

Just like with *cron*, *at* jobs will email any output from the script to the job owner, but it is often better to handle output within the shell script if possible.

Of course once you have scheduled jobs to run with *at,* you may find that you need to check when things are running or cancel a job. The command *atq* gives a simple way to check what is scheduled.

```
$ atq
6       2007-01-22 11:00 a oracle
5       2007-01-21 23:30 a oracle
```

The output of the *atq* command will vary between platforms but typically includes the job number, date and time that it is running, and the job owner. On some platforms the job number is an incremented number while on others it can appear almost random.

If you find you need to remove a scheduled job, you can use the *atrm* command, supplying the job number as an argument.

```
$ atrm 6
```

Using the *at* command to run tasks which must be run during non-business hours can keep you from having to work late or get up early, but care should be taken to make sure the jobs run properly.

Performing Tasks On Login

In chapter 3 we discussed the *.profile* (or *.bash_profile*) file which is executed every time a user logs in. This file is usually used to define variables that we want to have set up automatically every time we log in, but it can also be used to execute a script or command on login.

One potential use for running a command in the login file is to display information about the account as users log in. By adding the following line to the Oracle user's .profile file users can be given some information about the account they are logging into.

```
echo "This account should only be used by the database
administrator."
```

The output of any commands in the .profile is displayed to the screen of the user as they log in. In this example, we have simply echoed text to the screen; however, we could easily get more sophisticated.

```
echo "You are connected to the server `hostname`. The Oracle SID is
$ORACLE_SID."
```

This example will display the hostname and current SID on the screen at login. Useful information like backup times and the location of important files could also be included but we are not limited to just giving the user information. Entire shell scripts can be executed within the .profile.

Let's say each time we log into the machine we want to see the system uptime and load averages for the system. We can simply add the *uptime* command to the .profile and the output of the command will be displayed each time we log in.

By default, output will be written to the screen but could also be redirected to a log file. Any command or script can be run at login but there are a few pitfalls which should be avoided.

Commands and scripts in the .profile or .bash_profile files will be executed each time a user logs into that account. Since a user may log in multiple times without logging out you should make sure the script can safely be run multiple times.

You should also be careful to make sure you do not have a script in your .profile which relies on a variable or script which comes later in the .profile. For this reason I suggest setting variables (especially PATH) near the top of your .profile and executing other commands and shell scripts near the end.

Conclusion

In this chapter we have covered several techniques for automatically running scripts and commands. Cron is one of the most popular methods and it allows us to have scripts or commands run on a regular schedule based on time and date criteria.

While cron is best for jobs which need to be repeated at regular time intervals, the *at* scheduler was introduced as a way to run a job once at a certain date and time. This can be useful for scheduling things to run when the load on the system is lower or when it will not impact users.

By adding commands or scripts to the .profile or .bash_profile files we can automatically execute commands when a user logs in. While any command or script can be added to these files, this is most commonly used to display informational output to the user.

In the next chapter we will see some ways to make our scripts reach beyond a single user and even past a single machine. Through some of these advanced techniques we can allow users to safely execute commands as another user, move files between systems and monitor multiple systems.

Reaching Further

Moving files around, sending emails and executing commands on more than one system are just a few of the things we are going to cover in this chapter. It is all about making your shell scripts reach beyond a single file, just one database, or just one machine.

Transferring Files between Systems

Transferring files between machines is often necessary for backups, duplicating databases, moving files from development to production systems, and a host of other daily tasks. There are several tools which can be used for moving files around, each with their advantages and disadvantages. Here we will focus on the most flexible and secure tools available.

There are two tools which are typically available for securely transferring files between systems; *sftp* and *scp*. Both offer *ssh* protocol security but they work somewhat differently.

sftp - Secure FTP

While *sftp* is typically used interactively in the same way the *ftp* application would be used, it can also read commands from a file in batch mode. Here is an example of sftp being used interactively:

```
$ cd $ORACLE_HOME/network/admin
$ sftp sprog
Connecting to sprog...
Password: password
sftp> cd /u01/app/oracle/product/10.2.0/db_1/network/admin
```

```
sftp> put tnsnames.ora
Uploading tnsnames.ora to
/u01/app/oracle/product/10.2.0/db_1/network/admin/tnsnames.ora
tnsnames.ora                                100%  536     0.5KB/s
00:00
sftp> quit
```

These steps could be combined either into a separate batch file, using the -b option then giving the file name, or redirected into sftp on the command line in the same fashion we have been using for SQL*Plus.

```
#!/bin/bash
#
cd $ORACLE_HOME/network/admin
sftp sprog << EOF
cd /u01/app/oracle/product/10.2.0/db_1/network/admin
put tnsnames.ora
exit
EOF
```

This short shell script will now automatically perform all the steps, except entering the password, which we accomplished interactively before. The main commands within sftp are listed in the table below.

COMMAND	ACTION
quit bye	Close the connection and exit sftp (either command will work)
get	Retrieve a file from the remote system
put	Upload a file to the remote system
ls	List the contents of a directory on the local system. Many options which work with the *ls* command in the shell (like -l, -a and -t) also work with the *ls* command within sftp.
pwd	Show the current working directory on the remote system
cd	Change directory on the remote system
lpwd	Show the current working directory on the local system
lcd	Change directory on the local system
chmod	Change permissions of a given file
chown	Change ownership of a given file
chgrp	Change the group of a given file
rm	Remove a file from the remote system

COMMAND	ACTION
rmdir	Remove a directory from the remote system
help	Display the online help for sftp

Table 11.1: *sftp commands*

Many of these commands should be familiar and behave similarly to how they work in the shell. The ability to change permissions and ownership and to remove remote files and directories can be very useful in our shell scripts.

scp - Secure Copy

The *scp* command offers very similar functionality to the *cp* command used to copy files on the local system with the added advantage that it can connect to a remote system. For fairly straightforward moving of files between systems *scp* can offer the same security of *sftp* while simplifying the syntax.

```
$ scp $ORACLE_HOME/network/admin/tnsnames.ora \
sprog:/u01/app/oracle/product/10.2.0/db_1/network/admin/
Password: password
tnsnames.ora                              100%   536      0.5KB/s
00:00
```

The example above accomplishes the same as the previous *sftp* example but you can see that the syntax is simplified. Like *rm*, two files or locations are given as arguments in the order of source then destination. Either or even both file or location can contain a username followed by an at symbol (@) and a hostname followed by a colon (:). If the username is not specified the current username is used.

Let's take another example with *scp* where we want to copy a remote file owned by the user jemmons but we are logged in to the local system as oracle.

```
$ scp jemmons@sprog:~/chapter_11.txt ./
Password: password
chapter_11.txt                                  100%   73    0.1KB/s
00:00
```

By adding *jemmons@* to the source argument *scp* will connect to *sprog* as jemmons and prompt for that user's password. While we still cannot use variables which are set on the remote system (like $ORACLE_HOME) we can use the tilde (~) to indicate a user's home directory.

Below are the most commonly used arguments for *scp*:

OPTION	EFFECT
-p	Preserve modification time, access time and permissions of the original file
-r	Recursively copy directories and their contents
-q	Disable the progress meter

Table 11.2: *scp Arguments*

If either *sftp* or *scp* will work in a given situation it is often simpler to use *scp*, but when tasks like moving or renaming files become necessary the added flexibility of *sftp* becomes essential.

Executing commands on another system

Moving files from system to system is handy, but what if we want to execute commands on another system? Don't worry. We can use the familiar method of redirecting input with the *ssh* command to run commands remotely. In case you are not noticing the trend, we can do an awful lot by redirecting input into interactive commands.

Let's say we want to visually verify the hosts file on a remote system. Using *ssh* and redirected input we can have the script display the file from the remote system.

```
$ ssh sprog << EOF
> cat /etc/hosts
> exit
> EOF
Pseudo-terminal will not be allocated because stdin is not a
terminal.
Password: password
Sun Microsystems Inc.    SunOS 5.10      Generic January 2005
You have mail.
#
# Internet host table
#
127.0.0.1       localhost
192.168.1.4     sprog     loghost
192.168.1.3     glonk
$
```

After the commands are run, we are returned to the command prompt on the local system. The output of the *ssh* command can be redirected, with a greater-than symbol after the EOF file marker, but we need to keep in mind that it will be the entire output of the *ssh* session.

This is not the most efficient way to move text around, but using *ssh* in this fashion can be very helpful for coordinating tasks between systems. For instance, if we want to initiate an export on the system *glonk,* possibly just prior to copying the backup and performing a restore on the local system, we could use a script like the following:

```
#!/bin/bash
ssh glonk <<EOF
/u01/app/oracle/admin/oss/scripts/full_export.sh
exit
EOF
```

We could easily coordinate backups and restores between several machines in this way but we must always remain aware that when we execute commands remotely rather than on the local system we are introducing more potential points of failure. Now we need to be concerned that both systems need to be up and running as well as the network and ssh must be working properly on both systems. For most purposes these are acceptable risks, the key is to include logic in your shell script to handle these potential failures.

Keep Directories in Sync with rsync

Nearly every command we have used thus far will be standard on every UNIX and Linux system, *rsync* is not, but it is so useful for replicating and updating directory structures that it warrants inclusion.

rsync allows you to copy directories between systems in much the same way as *scp* (or *rcp*) but will then allow the incremental copy of only items which have changed. This is the operating system equivalent to taking an incremental RMAN backup of an Oracle database and restoring it onto a standby database.

rsync comes with many popular distributions of Linux and UNIX but if it is not already on your system do not fret. It is freely available as both source code and binary distribution for many popular operating systems at samba.anu.edu.au/rsync/. Root privileges will be needed to install *rsync*.

There is a long list of options to *rsync* which allow you to control how files get copied and updated. Here is a basic use of *rsync* to copy the contents of the /u01/app/oracle/admin/common directory, which is my preferred location for scripts which will be used on multiple databases, from the local system to the same location on the system named sprog. Like *scp*, *rsync* expects two arguments specifying the source and destination. Either can contain a username followed by an at symbol (@) or a hostname followed by a colon (:).

```
rsync -a --exclude logs --delete /u01/app/oracle/admin/common \
sprog:/u01/app/oracle/admin/common
```

This example shows some of the most common arguments for *rsync*. The *-a* (archive mode) argument actually has several effects on *rsync* including causing it to work recursively (copying subdirectories and their contents) and copying permissions, ownership, modification times, and even symlinks from the source to the destination.

The *--exclude* option tells *rsync* to exclude the logs directory from the synchronization, but this option could also be used to exclude an individual file. The *--delete* option forces *rsync* to delete files from the destination if they do not exist in the source.

Just like the *scp* command, *rsync* will prompt for a password. Since it is typically used in scheduled jobs rather than interactively *rsync* by default does not give much feedback.

By allowing you to copy only files which have changed, *rsync* can save a considerable amount of network bandwidth and time, but there is a tradeoff. *rsync* takes some time to figure out exactly what needs to be copied and on large, complex directory structures this can take many minutes or even hours before *rsync* even starts copying files. This is not typically a problem on directories with less than a thousand files but should be a consideration on larger directories.

Getting Past the Password Problem

In this chapter we have covered several methods for inter-machine operations all of which have one major flaw; they all require a password be entered. So how can we have a script run automatically, even unattended, if we have to be there to enter a password.

Thankfully the folks who developed the secure shell protocol thought of this. Ssh supports public-key authentication allowing users to generate an authentication key, place it in their home directory on a remote system, and then connect to that system without entering a password. While you may find methods to include a password in your script, like we do with Oracle passwords, these are unnecessary and less secure than key authentication.

Below is a typical setup of key-authenticated SSH. Some implementations may handle it differently and the commands and syntax will vary on some systems, but the basic steps should remain the same: confirm that the remote ("to") server has key authorization enabled, generate a new private/public key pair on the local ("from") machine and copy the public key to the authorized keys file on the remote system.

For key authentication to work it must be enabled in the SSH configuration for the system to which you are connecting. While that is a task for your system administrator, it is very simple to enable, typically just requiring the change of one line in the SSH daemon config file. Many systems have it enabled by default.

With key authentication enabled you are ready to set it up for the user. Log on to the system which will be initiating the ssh, scp, sftp or rsync connection with the account from which the command will be run. This will be the "from" system. On this system run the command below:

```
$ ssh-keygen -t rsa
Generating public/private rsa key pair.
Enter file in which to save the key (/home/oracle/.ssh/id_rsa):
<enter>
Enter passphrase (empty for no passphrase): <enter>
Enter same passphrase again: <enter>
Your identification has been saved in /home/oracle/.ssh/id_rsa.
Your public key has been saved in /home/oracle/.ssh/id_rsa.pub.
The key fingerprint is:
38:36:24:6e:f5:5e:3c:ec:75:c5:0a:35:a1:99:74:bd oracle@sprog
$ more .ssh/id_rsa.pub
```

```
ssh-rsa
AAAAB3NzaC1yc2EAAAABIwAAAIEA9h1A8GCI80eD69A4GJz3Gqfi5inNAJP30pVJXVuz
OcK1
rOKZMtsOCt2oXNxjsshxLGJbuz/L3SWEpyR5EiJOJ2jZ60j6qpKmlESkbP7rZtBabt+p
TGp2tio/CH04
TElsNs0pNAP4Ce6HS5pE9h1RdWgIC+qMKyiYygXar4sNPfE= oracle@sprog
```

The command *ssh-keygen* is used to create a public key and a private key. The location of these keys is printed to the screen. It could be changed at the prompt but unless you have a good reason to change it, you should accept the defaults.

Next the command asks for a passphrase. Leave the passphrase blank by typing enter twice. By entering no passphrase we are setting up a key pair which will not require user input to authenticate.

Now that the key pair has been generated we can copy the public key to the remote system. On the "to" system, change directory to your home directory and then into the .ssh directory. The .ssh directory will not appear in an *ls* listing unless you add the *-a* option. If this directory does not exist, you should create it. Open or create the *authorized_keys* file within the .ssh directory and paste in the exact text of the key from the .ssh/id_rsa.pub file on the "from" machine onto a new line.

Though the key will wrap over several lines on screen it is important that it all be on one line in the file. In *vi* you will know it is all on one line if you must use the left and right arrows to move through the key. Care should also be taken not to delete or destroy any keys already in the *authorized_keys* file.

You should now be able to use *ssh*, *scp*, *sftp*, *rsync* and any other commands which employ SSH for their secure communications. These steps only set up key authentication for connections initiating on the "from" machine. If you want to use key authentication both ways you will have to repeat these steps reversing the "to" and "from" machines.

> Despite not requiring a password, this method of key authentication is more secure than password authenticated SSH. It is important, however, to use this with care. Once set up anyone who has access to the "from" account will have access to the "to" account. This only becomes a concern where accounts are shared or publicly known, but should always be considered preferable to having passwords hard-coded in scripts or accounts without passwords.

Key authentication allows us to perform countless tasks securely without the need for hard-coded passwords or a user typing a password interactively. It only takes a few minutes to configure and allows a great amount of flexibility for remote command execution and file transfer between machines.

Executing Commands with Another User's Permissions

We have covered how to execute commands on a remote system, even as a different username on another system, but what if we want to execute a command on the current system but with another user's privileges?

One solution would be to connect to the current system thorough SSH. While secure, since we are working on the local system, there is generally no need for the overhead of SSH encryption. Another method employs *setuid* or *setgid* permissions. These would allow a command or script to run with the permissions of the owner rather than of the current user. Unfortunately, this method has been found to be insecure and is now disabled in many UNIX and Linux distributions.

The root user has the unusual ability to assume the identity of other users. While this is not something you want to take advantage of casually, it can be key to coordinating tasks, especially at startup and shutdown.

Using su to become Another User

If you are coordinating processes at system startup and shutdown, such as startup and shutdown of databases and other services, or otherwise have the need to control user processes as the root user, you can easily accomplish this with the *su* command. *su* allows a user to temporarily "become" another user, assuming their identity and all their permissions. Most UNIX and Linux systems will allow any user to use the *su* command, although some restrict the usage to certain privilege groups, but most users will have to provide the password for the user they are attempting to become.

```
$ whoami
oracle
$ su - jemmons
Password: password
$ whoami
jemmons
$ exit
```

Here the *whoami* command shows that we are currently connected as the user oracle. We then use the *su* command to assume the identity and permissions of the user jemmons. The *whoami* command confirms that we are now working as the user *jemmons*. We then use the *exit* command to return to life as oracle.

The dash (-) is optional. If present, it will cause the *su* command to source the .profile of the user or other login files as appropriate. The password given here is the password for the user jemmons.

The *su* command prompts for a password making it really only useful for an interactive shell session; however, when initiated by the root user *su* assumes the identity of the user provided without prompting for a password. This ability, combined with the *-c* option which allows us to specify a single command to be run, can allow us to coordinate tasks between multiple users as long as the root user is in command.

As an example, let's say we have a database and a web server on the same system that need to be started in order. Within a startup script we could place a *dbstart* command to be run from the oracle account followed by a command to start the http server.

```
#!/bin/bash
su - oracle -c dbstart
su - httpd -c 'apachectl start'
```

If run by root, this script will execute the *dbstart* command as oracle and, when that is done, run the *apachectl* command as the httpd user. The quotes around the second command are necessary because there is whitespace between the command and its option.

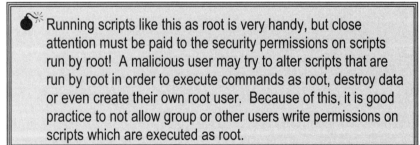

Running scripts like this as root is very handy, but close attention must be paid to the security permissions on scripts run by root! A malicious user may try to alter scripts that are run by root in order to execute commands as root, destroy data or even create their own root user. Because of this, it is good practice to not allow group or other users write permissions on scripts which are executed as root.

A script like this could be run as a non-root user, but the shell would prompt for the password for each user.

Emailing from scripts

There are several ways to send email from a script. The one you choose will depend on what tools you have on your system and how the script needs to notify you. Talk with your system administrator about how email is configured and what tools are available.

Emailing System Users and the .forward File

It is possible to send email to a user on the local system. If, for instance, email is sent to the user *oracle,* that user will be notified that they have a message upon their next login and they can then view the message with a mail reader present on the system.

```
$ mail oracle
Subject: Hello
Just a simple little note to say hello.
.
Cc:
```

Above we see the *mail* command being used interactively to send a short message to the *oracle* user. Since we are emailing a user on the same system on which we are executing the *mail* command there is no need to have the *@hostname.com* portion of the email address.

Emails which are sent to local addresses in this method go into the user's mail file and can be retrieved from the local system. That means, unless a *.forward* file is configured, someone has to regularly log into this system and check for emails.

In chapter 3 we covered how to configure the *.forward* file within a UNIX or Linux user's home directory. If a *.forward* file is present, rather than sending the email to the user's local mail file, the system will forward the email to each address listed in the

.forward file. This eliminates the need to regularly check for mail in system user's accounts.

Emails from cron and at Jobs

The *cron* daemon and *crontab* entries allow us to run commands and scripts on a regular schedule, even when we are not logged in. If a command or script is run and produces some output, the system places that output in an email and sends it to the owner of the script. Let's say this script is called from the oracle user's crontab file.

```
#!/bin/bash
df -h
```

Since there will be output to the *standard output* from this script, an email will be produced with the output in the body. The subject of the email may be blank, some generic message or may contain information about the job.

If there is a *.forward* file present, the output will be sent to the addresses listed. This may be the simplest way to produce an email from a shell script. It is often useful to set up scripts like this as a temporary measure until more sophisticated monitoring can be configured.

Any text sent to the *error output* is also emailed to the job owner. Even if you do not intend for your scripts to have any output to the standard output it is useful to have a *.forward* file, or check the accounts regularly, for errors from scheduled jobs.

Jobs scheduled using the *at* command will also send emails with any output from the commands run. If there is no output from commands, you can request that an email still be sent by adding the *-m* option to the *at* command when scheduling the job.

The mail command

While the automated emails from *cron* and *at* jobs offer a simple way to send emails, we can get a bit more sophisticated by using the *mail* command. Syntax for the mail command will vary between distributions and versions but the following offers a common use of the command.

```
#!/bin/bash
mail -s "Alert log from $ORACLE_SID `hostname`" oracle <
/u01/app/oracle/admin/$ORACLE_SID/bdump/alert_$ORACLE_SID.log
```

By using a redirect we have specified a file to be used as the body for this email. In this case we use a log file, but as we will see in other scripts, this could also be a file to which we have redirected other output. We also see how variables and commands can be used in the subject line.

For short messages, the mail command can also be used with file markers. Sometimes all we need to know is that a script has finished.

```
#!/bin/bash
mail -s "Script complete" oracle <<EOF
Script has completed
EOF
```

 On Solaris and some other System V based UNIX distributions, the *mail* command is used for different purposes. Because of this the *mailx* command was introduced with similar functionality to the *mail* command on other systems.

A typical method for sending email from a script is to compose the body of the message within a text file by redirecting output of specified commands into the file. The file is then easily redirected into the *mail* command and the subject added with the -*s* option.

It is often useful to put specifics in the subject line including host name, Oracle SID, and success or failure status messages. This can make it easier to automatically filter mail.

Conclusion

Before this chapter we mostly dealt with commands that only affected the system on which we ran them. In this chapter, we got a chance to go beyond that and see some methods that will allow us to monitor and manipulate things on other systems.

Transferring files between systems is very useful for creating backups of important files, but can also be used to distribute changes to files on multiple systems. The *sftp* and *scp* commands allow us to securely move files between machines.

We saw how commands can be executed on another system with the *ssh* command. This can be useful when tasks must be coordinated between systems.

The *rsync* command was introduced as a powerful method of synchronizing directories between systems. Though not always pre-installed on UNIX and Linux systems, when there is a need to do incremental updates to files and directories *rsync* can be very useful.

All of these methods require some type of authentication in order to function. Typically the commands will prompt for a password, but since we often want to be able to automate these commands we saw how key authentication can be used instead of passwords.

The *su* command allows us to temporarily assume the identity and privileges of another user if we know their password. The root user specifically has the ability to use this command without knowing the password allowing root to coordinate processes between different users.

Sending email to users on the system and optionally having that email forwarded to your preferred email address will be the main method of notification for our scheduled scripts. We saw how emails can automatically be generated by scheduled jobs and how we can use the *mail* command to generate custom emails.

Though it can be complex, inter-machine scripting can be very powerful and can help reduce the amount of maintenance administrators must perform manually. We will see these commands used heavily in the scripts throughout the rest of this book.

Oracle Database Maintenance

Any experienced Oracle administrator knows that there is a long list of things that need to be frequently monitored and maintained for a database to keep running smoothly. By automating these maintenance tasks we can effectively reduce the likelihood of human error and eliminate many of the more monotonous tasks.

Oracle has made an effort to automate some of these things in more recent versions of Oracle Database, but many of these conveniences come with the added burden of a GRID controller. While a couple of these scripts may seem obsolete, they are provided here for those who may not want the additional maintenance of a GRID controller and those who may be on older versions of Oracle which may not include the GRID controller.

Monitoring and Maintaining the Alert Log

The alert log is often the first place problems with a database will appear. By using shell scripts to monitor the alert log we are able to check it far more often than we ever would manually.

The jobs in this section should be run from the oracle user's crontab. You should choose the frequency that you think is appropriate for the specific database. I recommend rotating the alert log daily, but checking it at least every 15 minutes on

---

production databases. Since the scripts that check the alert log only notify you if there is a problem it is possible to run them more frequently, and some prefer every 5 minutes. Example crontab entries will be provided.

Checking for Errors in the Alert Log

The *check_alert_log.sh* script checks for any ORA- errors in the alert log of a given database. It will take a SID as an argument, or if no SID is specified, it will use the current one if set.

In order to avoid reporting the same error twice, this script will copy the contents out of the alert log, check for errors, and then save them in a log file by the same name, but with *.1* appended to it.

check_alert_log.sh

```bash
#!/bin/bash

# Add /usr/local/bin to the PATH variable so the oraenv command can
be found
PATH=$PATH:/usr/local/bin; export PATH

# If a SID is provided as an argument it will be set and oraenv run
# otherwise we will use the current SID.  If no SID is set or
provided
# an error message is displayed and the script exits with a status
of 1
if [ $1 ]
then
    ORACLE_SID=$1
    ORAENV_ASK=NO
    . oraenv
else
    if [ ! $ORACLE_SID ]
    then
        echo "Error: No ORACLE_SID set or provided as an
argument"
        exit 1
    fi
fi

# Set the ORACLE_BASE variable
ORACLE_BASE=/u01/app/oracle; export ORACLE_BASE
```

```
cd $ORACLE_BASE/admin/$ORACLE_SID/bdump

# Copy the current alert log into a temporary file and empty the
original
cp alert_$ORACLE_SID.log alert_$ORACLE_SID.log.temp
cp /dev/null alert_$ORACLE_SID.log

# Check the copy in the temporary file for ORA- errors
grep 'ORA-' alert_$ORACLE_SID.log.temp > /dev/null
# If found, email the Oracle user with the contents of the alert log
if [ $? = 0 ]
then
    mail -s "$ORACLE_SID database alert log error" oracle < \
          alert_$ORACLE_SID.log.temp
fi

# Move the contents of the temp file onto the permanent copy of the
log
# and remove the temp file.
cat alert_$ORACLE_SID.log.temp >> alert_$ORACLE_SID.log.1
rm alert_$ORACLE_SID.log.temp
```

The block of code that starts with the first if statement is one that we will see in many of the scripts in this book. If a SID is provided, the $1 variable exists and the *oraenv* command will be executed. If not, the second *if* statement within the *else* clause will check to see if a SID has already been set. If it has not, we will print an error message and exit the script with a result code of 1, indicating failure. If this script fails when executed from a crontab, the error message would automatically be emailed to the crontab owner.

Since this will likely be run from a crontab entry we will typically provide a SID as an argument. The following crontab entry will cause this script to be run every 15 minutes.

```
00,15,30,45 * * * * /u01/app/oracle/admin/common/check_alert_log.sh
oss
```

Rotating the Alert Log

This script should be considered a companion to the previous one. It will take the alert log created by the *check_alert_log.sh* script, which has a .1 appended on it, and rotate it out to a

---

tertiary alert log. The previous tertiary alert log is moved to a fourth alert log and so-on. The desired number of alert logs to keep can be set in the script by changing the value of the variable keep. The default of 7 should be fine for most databases.

🖫 rotate_alert_log.sh

```
#!/bin/bash

# The keep variable controls how many old alert logs should be kept
keep=7

# Add /usr/local/bin to the PATH variable so the oraenv command can
be found
PATH=$PATH:/usr/local/bin; export PATH

# If a SID is provided as an argument it will be set and oraenv run
# otherwise we will use the current SID.  If no SID is set or
provided
# an error message is displayed and the script exits with a status
of 1
if [ $1 ]
then
    ORACLE_SID=$1
    ORAENV_ASK=NO
    . oraenv
else
    if [ ! $ORACLE_SID ]
    then
            echo "Error: No ORACLE_SID set or provided as an
argument"
            exit 1
    fi
fi

# Set the ORACLE_BASE variable
ORACLE_BASE=/u01/app/oracle; export ORACLE_BASE

cd $ORACLE_BASE/admin/$ORACLE_SID/bdump

# Set the loop variable i to the keep value then rename each alert
log
# to one number up from its current value.  Stop after moving log 2
i=$keep
while [ $i -gt 2 ]
do
    if [ -e alert_$ORACLE_SID.log.`expr $i - 1` ]
    then
            mv alert_$ORACLE_SID.log.`expr $i - 1`
alert_$ORACLE_SID.log.$i
    fi
    i=`expr $i - 1`
done
```

```
# This handles the move of log 1.  If there is no log 1 an error
will be
# displayed and the script will exit with a status of 1.
if [ -e alert_$ORACLE_SID.log.1 ]
then
    mv alert_$ORACLE_SID.log.1 alert_$ORACLE_SID.log.2
    touch alert_$ORACLE_SID.log.1
else
    echo "File alert_$ORACLE_SID.log.1 not found"
    echo "Make sure you are using the check_alert_log.sh script"
    exit 1
fi
```

This script uses a *while loop* to work through a number of files without the need to repeat commands. The last file, which is the alert log ending with .1, is handled separately to allow an error to be raised if the file does not exist.

This script could be run at any interval. I would recommend running this script daily for active databases in order to keep the alert logs from growing too large. Weekly may be acceptable for databases that see less use. The crontab entry below shows how this script could be run daily. Note that it has been configured to run at five minutes after the hour in order to run at a time when the *check_alert_log.sh* script is most likely not running.

```
05 00 * * * /u01/app/oracle/admin/common/rotate_alert_log.sh oss
```

Finding and removing old dump files

Over time the files created in instances dump directories can consume quite a lot of space. Furthermore, since these typically grow slowly it is easy to forget to check them until they are large enough to cause a space problem. These reasons make this an ideal function for a shell script.

The *clean_dump_dirs.sh* shell script will check the adump, bdump, cdump and udump directories for a given database and remove any files older than 30 days. If you want to keep files in these directories for more or less time, you can change the value of the *days_back* variable to the desired number of days.

💾 clean_dump_dirs.sh

```
#!/bin/bash

# days_back should be set to how many days dump files should be kept
days_back=30

# Add /usr/local/bin to the PATH variable so the oraenv command can
be found
PATH=$PATH:/usr/local/bin; export PATH

# If a SID is provided as an argument it will be set and oraenv run
# otherwise we will use the current SID.  If no SID is set or
provided
# an error message is displayed and the script exits with a status
of 1
if [ $1 ]
then
    ORACLE_SID=$1
    ORAENV_ASK=NO
    . oraenv
else
    if [ ! $ORACLE_SID ]
    then
            echo "Error: No ORACLE_SID set or provided as an
argument"
            exit 1
    fi
fi

# Set the ORACLE_BASE variable
ORACLE_BASE=/u01/app/oracle; export ORACLE_BASE

# Clean the files matching both the name and modified time criteria
# out of each directory with a find command with an execute clause
find $ORACLE_BASE/admin/$ORACLE_SID/adump/ -name "*.aud" -mtime
+$days_back \
    -exec rm {} \;

find $ORACLE_BASE/admin/$ORACLE_SID/bdump/ -name "*.trc" -mtime
+$days_back \
    -exec rm {} \;

find $ORACLE_BASE/admin/$ORACLE_SID/cdump/ -name "*.trc" -mtime
+$days_back \
    -exec rm {} \;

find $ORACLE_BASE/admin/$ORACLE_SID/udump/ -name "*.trc" -mtime
+$days_back \
    -exec rm {} \;
```

Like the other scripts in this chapter, this script can be used with the current ORACLE_SID if it is set, or a SID can be provided as an argument. This script makes excellent use of the *find* command by checking for files that match both a name criteria and have a modification time of more than a certain number of days ago.

Older databases may not have an adump directory. If this is the case with your database, you can simply delete the lines which clean up the adump directory, or better yet, comment them out by adding a pound symbol at the beginning. Either way, make sure you get both lines of the command.

This script could be run daily, but weekly is probably sufficient. The following crontab entry will execute this script every Sunday morning at 1:00 am.

```
00 01 * * 0 /u01/app/oracle/admin/common/clean_dump_dirs.sh oss
```

Monitoring Tablespace Usage

When a tablespace fills up, the database will typically start posting ORA- errors to the alert log, but by then users are already encountering problems! It is far better if the DBAs know ahead of time that a tablespace is getting full. This script can be used to manually check tablespace usage. In chapter 14 we will see some scripts which can automatically check tablespace use and notify the administrator if space is low.

The *tablespace_usage.sh* script will print its output to the screen. It can be used on the current SID or a SID can be provided as an argument.

🖫 tablespace_usage.sh

```bash
#!/bin/bash

# Add /usr/local/bin to the PATH variable so the oraenv command can
be found
PATH=$PATH:/usr/local/bin; export PATH

# If a SID is provided as an argument it will be set and oraenv run
# otherwise we will use the current SID.  If no SID is set or
provided
# an error message is displayed and the script exits with a status
of 1
if [ $1 ]
then
    ORACLE_SID=$1
    ORAENV_ASK=NO
    . oraenv
else
    if [ ! $ORACLE_SID ]
    then
            echo "Error: No ORACLE_SID set or provided as an
argument"
            exit 1
    fi
fi

# Set the ORACLE_BASE variable
ORACLE_BASE=/u01/app/oracle; export ORACLE_BASE

# Here we enter SQL*Plus with the silent option, format the output
# and execute a query to check the tablespace usage
sqlplus -S "/ as sysdba" << EOF

set linesize 80
column percent_used format a12

select
    files.tablespace_name,
    files.size_in_mb,
    used.used_in_mb,
    round((used.used_in_mb/files.size_in_mb)*100) || '%' as
percent_used
from
    (
            select tablespace_name, round(sum(bytes)/1024/1024) as
size_in_mb
            from dba_data_files
            group by tablespace_name
    ) files,
    (
            select tablespace_name, round(sum(bytes)/1024/1024) as
used_in_mb
            from dba_extents
            group by tablespace_name
    ) used
```

```
where files.tablespace_name = used.tablespace_name
order by tablespace_name;

EOF
```

When run, the output of this script should look something like this:

```
$ ./tablespace_usage.sh

TABLESPACE_NAME                 SIZE_IN_MB USED_IN_MB PERCENT_USED
------------------------------- ---------- ---------- ------------
EXAMPLE                                100         68 68%
SYSAUX                                 390        379 97%
SYSTEM                                 490        487 99%
UNDOTBS1                                50         13 26%
USERS                                    5          3 60%
```

This script shows how SQL output can be seamlessly displayed to the screen. Each tablespace is listed with its size, the amount used, and the percentage of the tablespace that is used.

Clean Up Old Statspack Data

Oracle's statspack utility is very useful for collecting performance statistics on databases. The utility includes a script that can be used to purge old statspack data, but DBAs do not want the hassle of running this manually. Using the SQL script provided by Oracle this script will delete statspack data older than a certain number of days.

When calling the SQL script *sppurge.sql* in this shell script we use the special shortcut question mark (*?*) in describing the file location. When used in *sqlplus* the *?* gets expanded to the current database's Oracle home directory.

📇 **statspack**Error! Bookmark not defined.**_purge.sh**

```
#!/usr/bin/bash

# Set the number of days of statspack reports you want to keep
```

```
days_to_keep=90

# Define the location of the temporary file this script will use
tempfile=/tmp/statspack_purge_$ORACLE_SID.txt

# If a SID is provided as an argument it will be set and oraenv run
# otherwise we will use the current SID.  If no SID is set or
provided
# an error message is displayed and the script exits with a status
of 1
if [ $1 ]
then
    ORACLE_SID=$1
    ORAENV_ASK=NO
    . oraenv
else
    if [ ! $ORACLE_SID ]
    then
            echo "Error: No ORACLE_SID set or provided as an
argument"
            exit 1
    fi
fi

# Set the ORACLE_BASE variable
ORACLE_BASE=/u01/app/oracle; export ORACLE_BASE

# Read the perfstat user password from a pw file
perfstat_pw=`cat
$ORACLE_BASE/admin/$ORACLE_SID/passwords/perfstat.pw`

sqlplus -S perfstat/$perfstat_pw << EOF > $tempfile

    column minsnap new_value losnapid

    select min(snap_id) as minsnap
    from perfstat.stats\$snapshot;

    column maxsnap new_value hisnapid

    select max(snap_id) as maxsnap
    from perfstat.stats\$snapshot
    where snap_time < sysdate - $days_to_keep;

    @?/rdbms/admin/sppurge.sql

    exit

EOF

# Check the tempfile for ORA- erros and email oracle if any were
found
grep 'ORA-' $tempfile > /dev/null

if [ $? = 0 ]
then
```

```
      mail -s "Problem purging statspack data in $ORACLE_SID" oracle <
\
      $tempfile
fi

# Remove the temp file when we're done with it
rm $tempfile
```

The *sppurge.sql* script expects a *lowsnapid* and *hisnapid* variable to be set within sqlplus. This script uses the shell variable *days_to_keep* in a query that sets the *hisnapid* and the *losnapid* is set with a separate query. With these set, we can run the *sppurge.sql* script and exit. A temp file is used in this script but only so we can identify and report any errors that may happen during the SQL execution.

Statspack snapshots are usually taken on a regular schedule by an internal database job. If you are taking snapshots on an hourly basis, it is probably sufficient to clean out old snapshots once a week. The following crontab will run the statspack_purge.sh script every Sunday at 2 am.

```
00 02 * * 0 /u01/app/oracle/admin/common/statspack_purge.sh oss
```

This process can be time consuming and will take a large amount of temp space if it is cleaning a large number of reports. It should be run on a regular basis and at a time when database usage is low.

Check Certain Database Accounts are Locked

For the highest level of security it is often wise to lock certain accounts within a database. For instance you may want to lock the accounts which own the important tables in your database and grant only minimal privileges to the users which must access them. Since these accounts will often need to be unlocked for upgrades it is handy to have a script check to make sure they have been locked again afterwards.

🖫 audit_locked_accounts.sh

```
#!/usr/bin/bash

# If a SID is provided as an argument it will be set and oraenv run
# otherwise we will use the current SID.  If no SID is set or
provided
# an error message is displayed and the script exits with a status
of 1
if [ $1 ]
then
    ORACLE_SID=$1
    ORAENV_ASK=NO
    . oraenv
else
    if [ ! $ORACLE_SID ]
    then
        echo "Error: No ORACLE_SID set or provided as an
argument"
        exit 1
    fi
fi

# Define the location of the temporary file this script will use
tempfile=/tmp/audit_locked_accounts_$ORACLE_SID.txt

# Start sqlplus and check for locked accounts
sqlplus -S "/ as sysdba" << EOF > $tempfile

    set pagesize

    select 'The following accounts were found to be unlocked and
should not be'
    from dual;

    define exit_status = 0

    column xs new_value exit_status

    select username, account_status, 1 as xs from dba_users
    where account_status != 'LOCKED'
    and username in ('HR', 'SCOTT', 'OUTLN', 'MDSYS', 'CTXSYS');

    exit &exit_status

EOF

# If the exit status of sqlplus was not 0 then we will send an email
if [ $? != 0 ]
then
    mail -s "Accounts Unlocked in $ORACLE_SID" oracle < $tempfile
fi

rm $tempfile
```

To use this script you will want to change the usernames listed in the SQL query. This uses a similar method to the *tablespace_usage_alert.sh* script to email the Oracle user if accounts are found to be unlocked.

Though it could be run more often this script is typically run daily. This crontab entry will run the *audit_locked_accounts.sh* script every morning at 2:15 am.

```
15 02 * * * /u01/app/oracle/admin/common/audit_locked_accounts.sh
oss
```

Cleaning Old Data Out of Tables

Typically there are a couple tables in the database that will grow constantly and eventually need pruning. A good example of this would be a table which tracks logins. Since Oracle does not come with this functionality, an SQL script called *session_audit_setup.sql* that will create such a table and triggers to populate it is included in the code depot. This type of script can be easily modified for other tables of this sort.

Many parts of the script should be familiar by now. This script will handle a SID being passed as an argument, but can also take a second argument of how many days of data to keep. The first *if* statement in the script checks to see if the second argument was provided and if it was it will use that for the *days_to_keep* variable. If the second argument was not provided, the script will use the default of 180 days.

🖫 session_audit_cleanup.sh

```
#!/bin/bash

# Set the number of days of old data to keep
# If a second parameter is given it will be used for the number of
days to keep
```

```
if [ $2 ]
then
    days_to_keep=$2
else
    days_to_keep=180
fi

# If a SID is provided as an argument it will be set and oraenv run
# otherwise we will use the current SID.  If no SID is set or
provided
# an error message is displayed and the script exits with a status
of 1
if [ $1 ]
then
    ORACLE_SID=$1
    ORAENV_ASK=NO
    . oraenv
else
    if [ ! $ORACLE_SID ]
    then
            echo "Error: No ORACLE_SID set or provided as an
argument"
            exit 1
    fi
fi

# Define the location of the temporary file this script will use
tempfile=/tmp/session_audit_cleanup_$ORACLE_SID.txt

# Start sqlplus and check for locked accounts
sqlplus -S "/ as sysdba" << EOF > $tempfile

    delete from sys.session_audit where logon_time < sysdate -
$days_to_keep;

    commit;

    exit;

EOF

# If errors are found in the tempfile then email the oracle user
grep 'ORA-' $tempfile
if [ $? = 0 ]
then
    mail -s "Problem cleaning session_audit in $ORACLE_SID" oracle <
$tempfile
fi

rm $tempfile
```

Adding the option to override a default value with an argument can help reduce your overall number of scripts. If, for instance, you want to keep database logon information for 180 days in production, but 30 days is sufficient for developing, you can easily use this script for either without the need to customize it.

The following crontab entries show how the script can be used with the default on the oss database and with the added argument of 30 days on the dev database. Both run daily.

```
15 02 * * * /u01/app/oracle/admin/common/session_audit_cleanup.sh
oss
15 02 * * * /u01/app/oracle/admin/common/session_audit_cleanup.sh
dev 30
```

Execute a SQL Script on Every Database

There may be times when you need to execute the same script on all the databases on a host. This script will loop through the /etc/oratab file and run the provided SQL script (given as an argument.)

The *execute_onall_dbs.sh* script requires two arguments. First, you must provide database connection information. You could provide it in the form of a username/password pair in quotes or you could specify "/ as sysdba". The second argument will be the SQL script you wish to run.

This script will ask before applying the provided script to each database unless an optional third argument of 'noprompt' is given.

🖫 execute_on_all_dbs.sh

```
#!/bin/bash

# If there aren't at least two arguments something is wrong and we
should
# exit with an error and suggested usage information
if [ ! $2 ]
then
    echo "Usage: execute_on_all_dbs.sh 'username/password' \
scriptname.sql noprompt (optional)"
```

```
      exit 99
fi

# Transfer arguments into more meaningful variable names and set a
default
# if the third argument was not specified.
connect_string=$1
scriptname=$2
if [ $3 ]
then
    prompt=$3
else
    prompt=yesprompt
fi

ORAENV_ASK=NO

# For each database defined in the /etc/oratab file
for sid in `grep -v '#' /etc/oratab | egrep -v '^\s*$' | cut -f1 -
d':'`
do
# Unless noprompt was given as the third argument we will ask before
applying
# the given script to each database
    if [ ! $prompt = 'noprompt' ]
    then
            yesno=N
            while [ $yesno = 'N' ]
            do
                    echo "Execute $scriptname on $sid? (Y/N)"
                    read yesno
                    if [ $yesno = 'N' -o $yesno = 'Y' ]
                    then
                            break
                    else
                            echo "Input not recognized, please answer
Y or N."
                            yesno=N
                    fi
            done
    else
            yesno=Y
    fi

# If the answer to the prompt was Y or noprompt was set we will
# set up the environment, call sqlplus and execute the script
    if [ $yesno = 'Y' ]
    then
            ORACLE_SID=$sid
            . oraenv

            sqlplus -S $connect_string <<EOF
            @$scriptname
EOF
    fi
done
```

The *execute_on_all_dbs.sh* script is quite a bit more complex than the previous ones in this chapter. Because of this, the first thing the script does is check to make sure at least two arguments have been provided. If they have not, the script will print some helpful output to the screen and exit immediately. If enough arguments are provided, the script will transfer their contents from the default variables ($1, $2, etc.) to variables with more meaningful names. This step only serves to make the script more readable.

The *for loop* in this script will parse over each database on the current system. This is accomplished by extracting the database SIDs from the /etc/oratab file by first excluding comments (lines with a pound symbol) and blank lines, then taking only the first column of the remaining lines. The *for loop* will repeat the steps for each database, each time changing the sid script variable to a differed SID from the /etc/oratab file.

Within the for loop the user is prompted to confirm the given script should be applied to each database (unless noprompt has been specified) and, if they have answered 'Y', sqlplus is called and the script executed. When these steps have been repeated for each database the for loop ends and the script is complete.

The *execute_on_all_dbs.sh* script will use the same username and password for each database so it is important that these be in synch. Here are two potential uses for the script.

```
$ ./execute_on_all_dbs.sh "/ as sysdba" @?/rdbms/admin/utlrp.sql
Execute @?/rdbms/admin/utlrp.sql on oss? (Y/N)
Y

TIMESTAMP
----------------------------------------------------------------
-----------
COMP_TIMESTAMP UTLRP_BGN  2007-02-19 16:34:05
```

```
PL/SQL procedure successfully completed.

...

PL/SQL procedure successfully completed.

Execute @?/rdbms/admin/utlrp.sql on dev? (Y/N)
N
$ ./execute_on_all_dbs.sh "scott/tiger" @myscript.sql noprompt
$
```

The first example prompts before running the SQL script on each database. The second shows how the script can be used with the noprompt argument. Any output from the script will be printed to the screen; however, the printing of prompts has been suppressed with the -S option to sqlplus.

Copy the TNSNames File to a List of Systems

It can really be a pain to update the TNSNames file on every system when you add, move or remove a database. If your Oracle home is in the same location on each system (which I highly recommend) this script can take a lot of the hassle out of updating tnsnames.ora.

Instead of taking a list of arguments, this script looks for a file called *db_hosts* in the /u01/app/oracle/admin/common directory. The *db_hosts* file should consist of a list of server names which the file should be distributed to each on their own line. If you want to keep a list of hosts in a different location you can just change the *db_host_file* variable definition in the script.

distribute_tnsnames.sh

```
#!/bin/bash

# This script assumes your ORACLE_HOME directory is the same on all
systems

# Set the db_hosts file to the file listing which host's tnsnames
should be
# distributed then confirm the file is readable
```

```
db_host_file=/u01/app/oracle/admin/common/db_hosts
if [ ! -r $db_host_file ]
then
    echo "The list of database hosts is either missing or not
readable."
    exit 99
fi

# If the ORACLE_HOME variable is not set display an error and exit
if [ ! $ORACLE_HOME ]
then
    echo "No ORACLE_HOME set! Please set ORACLE_HOME and try again."
    exit 99
fi

# For each hostname defined in the db_hosts file
for host in `cat $db_host_file`
do
    echo "Transferring the TNS Names file to $host"
# Copy the TNS Names file to each host
    scp $ORACLE_HOME/network/admin/tnsnames.ora \
    $host:$ORACLE_HOME/network/admin/tnsnames.ora
done
```

The *for loop* in this script is less complex than in the last one and demonstrates how items listed in a text file can easily be used as input for a shell script. My db_hosts file for this script looks like this:

```
sprog
glonk
jemmons@splunge
db.lifeaftercoffee.com
```

Here I have hosts listed as just the hostname, the hostname with username, and a fully qualified domain name. Anything that *scp* will accept is fine here, but if no username is specified the current one will be used.

If key authentication is configured for these systems the files will be copied without the user entering a password. This is ideal, but not necessary. If key authentication is not configured the script will simply prompt for a password.

This script could easily be adapted to distribute a new .profile file or other configuration files. In the next chapter we will see how a script can keep an entire directory in sync with *rsync*, but for individual files *scp* will suffice.

Conclusion

This chapter is really where the "rubber hits the road" as far as scripts goes. Scripts in this chapter covered many of the common tasks of the Oracle DBA.

Scripts were shown to monitor and rotate the alert logs. While fairly simple, these scripts help relieve the administrator of the task of checking the logs frequently.

Cleaning up the dump directories is a more occasional task, but one which is easily handled by a shell script. The script provided can easily remove files older than a certain number of days from several directories.

Three different scripts were shown to help monitor tablespace usage. The first prints usage information to the screen, the second emails a similar usage report and the third is used to alert the DBA only when free space drops below a certain percentage.

Oracle's statspack utility, when active, creates a large amount of data. A script was provided to automatically trim back the statspack records to a certain number of days.

As a simple form of security auditing, a script was provided that will check to see if certain database accounts are locked. This is a nice check to run if you typically keep schema owners and other important accounts locked.

Many applications will keep a log or audit trail in tables in the database. A cleanup script is often necessary to keep these tables from growing indefinitely. A simple cleanup script was provided which could be easily modified for a specific application.

No one likes to run the same thing more than once, so a shell script was provided which executes a SQL script on every database on the system. The script optionally prompts for confirmation that the script should be run on each database.

Copying TNS Names and other configuration files to all your database servers can also be tedious so we saw how a script can parse through a file containing a list of hosts and transfer the TNS Names file to each.

These scripts should work on your system with little to no modification, but they should also be used as a platform for expanding upon. Consider the following ideas and how you might use them in your own shell scripts:

- Checking a file for certain text
  - see check_alert_log.sh
- Searching by file attribute and executing commands on found files
  - see clean_dump_dirs.sh
- Integrating SQL results on the command line
  - see tablespace_usage.sh
- Sending SQL output via email
  - see tablespace_usage_report.sh
- Use SQL results to determine if something is wrong
  - See tablespace_usage_alert.sh and audit_locked_accounts.sh

- Use a list from a file in a shell script

  - See execute_on_all_dbs.sh and distribute tnsnames.sh

Always make sure you test any script on a development system and database before using it in production, but don't be afraid to experiment.

The next chapter will focus on the ever important backup and recovery. More example scripts and crontab entries will be provided, so if you're ready, let's go!

Backup Scripts

Database backups are what we DBAs lose sleep over at night. Are the backups valid? Are they happening at the right time? Are they even still running? Even the most robust script can occasionally fail, but if they are set up right you can almost guarantee you will be notified if they do.

If you are scheduling your backups with cron (as most of us do) it is very important you set up a .forward file for the oracle user. Most of the scripts presented here do not print output to standard out, but if there is a problem, such as a command or file not found error, these will be sent to the error output which will be emailed to the oracle user.

Cold Backups without RMAN

When it is possible to take a database down for backup, a complete cold backup of the database offers a very clean way to recover the database to a certain point in time. This can be handy immediately before an upgrade or just prior to a hardware change.

With this script, we can specify a SID or if one is set in the current environment, use that one. Much of the output is sent to a log file which is eventually emailed to the Oracle user.

🖫 cold_backup.sh

```
#!/bin/bash

# Add /usr/local/bin to the PATH variable so the oraenv command can
be found
PATH=$PATH:/usr/local/bin; export PATH

# If a SID is provided as an argument it will be set and oraenv run
# otherwise we will use the current SID.  If no SID is set or
provided
# an error message is displayed and the script exits with a status
of 1
if [ $1 ]
then
    ORACLE_SID=$1
    ORAENV_ASK=NO
    . oraenv
else
    if [ ! $ORACLE_SID ]
    then
        echo "Error: No ORACLE_SID set or provided as an
argument"
        exit 1
    fi
fi

ORACLE_BASE=/u01/app/oracle; export ORACLE_BASE

admin_dir=$ORACLE_BASE/admin/$ORACLE_SID; export admin_dir

# Backup variables.  Set the backup_dir to the appropriate
# location for your site.
backup_dir=/u01/backup/cold/$ORACLE_SID; export backup_dir
log_file=$admin_dir/scripts/cold_backup_$ORACLE_SID.log

# Change directory to the script dir
cd $admin_dir/scripts

# This adds some text and a date stamp to the beginning of the
backup log
echo "Beginning cold backup of $ORACLE_SID" > $log_file
date >> $log_file

# Generate the cold backup script, shutdown the database,
# run the generated script and startup again.
sqlplus -S "/ as sysdba" << EOF >> $log_file

set pagesize
set linesize 1000

spool file_copy_$ORACLE_SID.sh

select 'cp ' || name || ' $backup_dir/' from v\$controlfile;
```

```
select 'cp ' || file_name || ' $backup_dir/' from dba_data_files;

select 'cp ' || member || ' $backup_dir/' from v\$logfile;

spool off

shutdown immediate;

!bash file_copy_$ORACLE_SID.sh

startup;

exit

EOF

rm file_copy_$ORACLE_SID.sh

# Backup key files if they are present
if [ -e $ORACLE_HOME/dbs/init$ORACLE_SID.ora ]
then
    cp $ORACLE_HOME/dbs/init$ORACLE_SID.ora $backup_dir/
fi

if [ -e $ORACLE_HOME/dbs/spfile$ORACLE_SID.ora ]
then
    cp $ORACLE_HOME/dbs/spfile$ORACLE_SID.ora $backup_dir/
fi

if [ -e $ORACLE_HOME/dbs/orapw$ORACLE_SID ]
then
    cp $ORACLE_HOME/dbs/orapw$ORACLE_SID $backup_dir/
fi

# Add some end text and timestamp to the log file
echo "Finished cold backup of $ORACLE_SID" >> $log_file
date >> $log_file

# Email appropriate folks
mail -s "$ORACLE_SID Cold Backup Complete" oracle < $tempfile
```

This script uses a spool file within SQL*Plus to create a dynamic shell script. The shell script is then executed directly from SQL*Plus by using the exclamation point (!) to execute the shell command *bash*.

The script also checks for several critical files and, if they are present, they will be copied to the backup directory. Finally the log file is emailed to the Oracle user.

Hot Backups without RMAN

Hot backups are far more commonplace and this script offers a good starting point for implementing hot backups if your site does not use rman. Keep in mind that this script should be considered a starting point only! This script does not back up your archive logs and you will need them for recovery!

Like the cold backup script, *hot_backup.sh* creates a command file by spooling SQL results to a file. Instead of script commands this script generates a series of SQL commands with script commands in-line.

hot_backup.sh (partial script shown)

```
#!/bin/bash

...

# Generate the hot backup script and run it
sqlplus -S "/ as sysdba" << EOF >> $log_file

alter database backup controlfile to
'$backup_dir/backup_controlfile.ctl';

set pagesize
set linesize 1000

column tablespace_name noprin
column sortorder noprin
column textout format a120

spool hot_backup_$ORACLE_SID.sql

select tablespace_name,
'1' sortorder,
'alter tablespace '|| tablespace_name ||' begin backup;' textout
from dba_data_files
union
select tablespace_name,
'2' sortorder,
'host cp '||file_name||' '||'$backup_dir' textout
from dba_data_files
union
select tablespace_name,
'3' sortorder,
'alter tablespace '||tablespace_name ||' end backup;' textout
```

```
from dba_data_files
order by tablespace_name, sortorder, textout;

select 'alter system archive log current;' from dual;

spool off

@hot_backup_$ORACLE_SID.sql

exit

EOF

. . .
```

Most of this script is the same as the cold backup script, but instead of individual commands, sets of commands are spooled out to the SQL script. A set like the following is created for each datafile in the database. When the script is run, each tablespace will be put into backup mode, copied to the backup directory, and then the tablespace is brought out of backup mode.

```
alter tablespace EXAMPLE begin backup;
host cp /u01/app/oracle/product/10.2.0/oradata/oss/example01.dbf
/u01/backup/oss/hot
alter tablespace EXAMPLE end backup;
```

Some hot backup scripts will put all tablespaces into backup mode before starting the backup, but by handling one tablespace at a time this script minimizes the impact on transactions in the database.

The frequency of backups will be a product of the size of the database, rate of change, usage cycle and time-to-recovery needs. While these topics are beyond the scope of this book, suffice it to say that most choose to back up their databases daily or weekly. The crontab below represents a daily backup of the oss database and a weekly backup of the dev database. The backup of the oss database is at 3:15 daily, but the backup of the dev database has been scheduled for 4:15 on Sunday morning so it will not cause excessive simultaneous writes.

```
15 03 * * * /u01/app/oracle/admin/common/scripts/hot_backup.sh oss
15 04 * * 0 /u01/app/oracle/admin/common/scripts/hot_backup.sh dev
```

Hot Backups with RMAN

Oracle's RMAN (Recovery MANager) utility was introduced in Oracle 8i as a new and better way to back up databases. In its initial versions, it was tedious to configure, but each version since has brought improvements in usability and new features.

Since version 9iR2 RMAN has been my preferred option for database backup. Configuration of RMAN is beyond the scope of this book, but once configured RMAN can be used with EOF file markers in a similar way to how we have been using them with SQL*Plus.

The hot and cold backup scripts presented earlier in this chapter use SQL*Plus to connect "/ as sysdba" but this script expects the password to be in a file in the admin directory. By transferring the value into a variable, the script also avoids the password displaying in a *ps* process listing.

🖫 rman_hot_backup.sh (partial script shown)

```
#!/bin/bash

# Add /usr/local/bin to the PATH variable so the oraenv command can
be found
PATH=$PATH:/usr/local/bin; export PATH

# A second argument can be provided to give a backup level
# if the backup level is not provided a level 0 backup will be
performed.
if [ $2 ]
then
    backup_level=$2
else
    backup_level=0
fi

# If a SID is provided as an argument it will be set and oraenv run
# otherwise we will use the current SID.  If no SID is set or
provided
# an error message is displayed and the script exits with a status
of 1
```

```
if [ $1 ]
then
    ORACLE_SID=$1
    ORAENV_ASK=NO
    . oraenv
else
    if [ ! $ORACLE_SID ]
    then
        echo "Error: No ORACLE_SID set or provided as an
argument"
        exit 1
    fi
fi

ORACLE_BASE=/u01/app/oracle; export ORACLE_BASE

admin_dir=$ORACLE_BASE/admin/$ORACLE_SID; export admin_dir

backup_user=backup_admin
backup_user_pw=`cat
$ORACLE_BASE/admin/$ORACLE_SID/pw/$backup_user.pw`

catalog_user=rman
catalog_user_pw=`cat
$ORACLE_BASE/admin/$ORACLE_SID/pw/$catalog_user.pw`

# Backup variables.  Set the backup_dir to the appropriate
# location for your site.
log_file=$admin_dir/scripts/rman_hot_backup_$ORACLE_SID.log

# This adds some text and a date stamp to the beginning of the
backup log
echo "Beginning hot backup of $ORACLE_SID" > $log_file
date >> $log_file

rman target=$backup_user/$backup_user_pw \
catalog=$catalog_user/$catalog_user_pw@rman <<EOF >> $log_file

backup incremental level=$BACKUP_LEVEL database plus archivelog
delete input;

delete noprompt obsolete;

quit;

EOF

# Add some end text and timestamp to the log file
echo "Finished hot backup of $ORACLE_SID" >> $log_file
date >> $log_file

# Email appropriate folks only if an error is found
grep "ORA-" $log_file > /dev/null
ora_err=$?
grep "RMAN-" $log_file > /dev/null
rman_err=$?
```

```
if [ $ora_err = 0 -o $rman_err = 0 ]
then
    mail -s "$ORACLE_SID Hot Backup Problem" oracle < $log_file
fi
```

This script will take a SID as the first argument then, if a second argument is supplied, it will be used as the backup level. If not specified a level 0 (full) backup is performed.

Most of the configuration (including backup location) is done when RMAN is set up so we only need to issue a few commands here. The script could be further simplified by combining the RMAN commands into RMAN scripts. While this is a convenient way to combine RMAN commands it is much more difficult to maintain than just changing a shell script.

This script checks the log file for ORA- or RMAN- errors. After checking for each, it captures the result code from the *grep* command. These result codes are used in a complex condition which will trigger an email to be sent if either ORA- or RMAN- errors are found.

RMAN allows the flexibility of performing a full (level 0) backup or incremental (levels 1-9) backups. Incremental backups will capture all data which has changed since the last backup of a lower level. By specifying the backup level with this script it is easy to take a bi-weekly full backup and appropriate incremental backups daily.

The following crontab entries take a full backup on Sundays and Wednesdays at 3:15 am, and then level 1 on Monday, Tuesday, and Thursday through Saturday. By specifying multiple days with date ranges it is possible to minimize the number of crontab entries needed to accomplish this.

```
15 03 * * 0,3 /u01/app/oracle/admin/common/scripts/hot_backup.sh oss
0
```

```
15 03 * * 1-2,4-6 /u01/app/oracle/admin/common/scripts/hot_backup.sh
oss 1
```

Database and Schema Export

Oracle's *exp* and *imp* commands offer the ability to use a parameter file. While parameter files are convenient, the syntax is still somewhat cumbersome. By initiating the *exp* and *imp* commands through a shell script we can simplify the syntax and take advantage of setting some defaults.

The key to this script's flexibility is the ability to accept arguments. If the arguments are not provided, logical defaults are set.

exp arguments which should always be applied (such as STATISTICS=NONE) can be added to the *exp_arguments* variable in this script.

🖫 dba_full_export.sh

```
#!/bin/bash

exp_arguments='USERID="/ as sysdba" BUFFER=10485760 FULL=Y'

# Add /usr/local/bin to the PATH variable so the oraenv command can
be found
PATH=$PATH:/usr/local/bin; export PATH

# If a SID is provided as an argument it will be set and oraenv run
# otherwise we will use the current SID.  If no SID is set or
provided
# an error message is displayed and the script exits with a status
of 1
if [ $1 ]
then
    ORACLE_SID=$1
    ORAENV_ASK=NO
    . oraenv
else
    if [ ! $ORACLE_SID ]
    then
        echo "Error: No ORACLE_SID set or provided as an
argument"
        exit 1
```

```
      fi
fi

ORACLE_BASE=/u01/app/oracle

log_file=$ORACLE_BASE/admin/$ORACLE_SID/scripts/dba_full_export_$ORA
CLE_SID.log

# If a second argument was specified use it as the file destination
if [ $2 ]
then
    exp_arguments="$exp_arguments FILE=$2"
else
    exp_arguments="$exp_arguments
FILE="$ORACLE_SID"_full_export.dmp"
fi

# Put some informational text in the log file
echo "Starting export `date`" > $log_file
echo "Exporting with the following arguments: $exp_arguments" >>
$log_file

# Run the export with the arguments provided and capture the result
code
exp $exp_arguments >> $log_file 2>&1

exp_result=$?

echo "Completed export `date`" >> $log_file

# Email appropriate folks only if an error is found
if [ exp_result != 0 ]
then
    mail -s "$ORACLE_SID Export Problem" oracle < $log_file
fi
```

A log file is specified in this script and some informational text as well as the output of the *exp* command is written to the log. Since *exp* writes information to the *standard error* output this script uses the redirect *2>&1* to cause the information to also be written to the log file.

The *exp_arguments* variable is initiated with some default values that are then, if a second argument was specified when the script was called, added to the variable. When the export command is executed we use the *exp_argument* variable to include all the arguments we need. We'll see more of this in the upcoming export scripts.

The following cron entry would take a weekly export of the oss database to the /u01/backup/oss/export directory.

```
00 04 * * 0 /u01/app/oracle/admin/common/scripts/dba_full_export.sh
oss /u01/backup/oss/full_export.dmp
```

The *dba_schema_export.sh* script allows an individual schema to be exported. Like the *dba_export.sh* script it connects "/ as sysdba" and therefore a password is not needed.

The schema is specified as the second argument to the script. An optional third argument is used to specify a file location.

🖫 dba_schema_export.sh (partial script shown)

```
#!/bin/bash

exp_arguments='USERID="/ as sysdba" BUFFER=10485760 FULL=N'

...

schema=$2

log_file=$ORACLE_BASE/admin/$ORACLE_SID/scripts/dba_schema_export_$O
RACLE_SID_$schema.log

exp_arguments="$exp_arguments OWNER=$schema"

# If a third argument was specified use it as the file destination
if [ $3 ]
then
    exp_arguments="$exp_arguments FILE=$3"
else
    exp_arguments="$exp_arguments
FILE="$ORACLE_SID"_"$schema"_export.dmp"
fi

...
```

The arguments are handled similarly to the way they were in the *dba_full_export.sh* script. With a bit more logic it would be possible to combine these scripts, but I prefer more simple scripts to a few complex ones.

Database and Schema Export

Conclusion

As mentioned at the beginning of this chapter, since every environment is different, your backup needs will vary. That having been said, we have seen some working examples of backup scripts that will help you put together scripts that meet your needs.

Traditionally cold or hot backups were done by hand or with shell scripts. There is still value to taking an extra cold backup before a major upgrade. It can offer an extra recovery option in case things go wrong.

Hot backups, where the database is available for query and transactions during the backup, are far more common. They can be accomplished with a minimal impact with a dynamic shell script.

Oracle's RMAN utility will take care of the hard work for you when it comes to backups, but it is still handy to have a shell script in control. We saw how a shell script can execute a series of RMAN commands and handle the output appropriately.

Finally we saw how shell scripts can be used to simplify the use of the *exp* command. Since this command typically requires a lot of arguments (including username/password, file, schema information) it is nice to have a shell script to control these.

Note that none of these scripts alone represent a complete backup solution! Furthermore, any backup solution should be tested on a regular basis. This is often overlooked, but is the only way to be truly confident in your backups.

In the next chapter we'll look at how we can monitor certain aspects of the Oracle database to make sure things are running well.

Oracle Database Monitoring

There is no shortage of things you need to keep an eye on in an Oracle database. In this chapter, we will look at how we can automate some of this monitoring and alert the administrator, run a command to fix the problem, or both.

Listener Availability

For all intents of purpose if the listener to your database is down, the database is down. In this script we use the lsnrctl command to check the status of the listener. If it is running, everything is fine and the script exits. If it is down the script will attempt to start the listener and email the oracle user.

🖫 check_listener.sh

```
#!/bin/bash

# If a SID is provided as an argument it will be set and oraenv run
# otherwise we will use the current SID.  If no SID is set or
provided
# an error message is displayed and the script exits with a status
of 1
if [ $1 ]
then
    ORACLE_SID=$1
    ORAENV_ASK=NO
    . oraenv
else
    if [ ! $ORACLE_SID ]
    then
        echo "Error: No ORACLE_SID set or provided as an
argument"
        exit 1
    fi
fi
```

```
# Define the location of the temporary file this script will use
tempfile=/tmp/check_listener_$ORACLE_SID.txt

lsnrctl status > $tempfile

if [ $? != 0 ]
then
    echo "Listener problem, attempting to start listener" >>
$tempfile
    lsnrctl start >> $tempfile
    if [ $? = 0 ]
    then
        mail -s "Listener restarted for $ORACLE_SID" oracle <
$tempfile
    else
        mail -s "Listener down, problems restarting for
$ORACLE_SID" \
            oracle < $tempfile
    fi
fi

rm $tempfile
```

This script uses the exit status from the lsnrctl command to determine the success or failure of the command. If *lsnrctl status* returns a *0* we know the command ran successfully and the listener is running. In this case the script does not send any notifications, instead just removes the temp file.

If, however, the lsnrctl has a non-zero exit status we know there is trouble. The script will then execute a *lsnrctl start* command and send an email. Notice that the subject of the email will vary depending on the exit status of *lsnrctl start*. The body of the email will contain the contents of the temp file and therefore will have the output of the listener status and start commands.

A SID is taken as an argument only so we may use the oraenv command to set the Oracle home directory and add the Oracle binaries to the path. Nothing about the database is checked with this script. That will be handled in the next section.

Checking the listener every 15 minutes will be sufficient for most purposes. Remember that the script should have a SID given as an argument.

```
00,15,30,45 * * * * /u01/app/oracle/admin/common/check_listeners.sh
oss
```

Database Availability

Having a working listener gets you through the door, but next you will want to make sure you can connect to a database. The first script can be used to check a local database. It uses the familiar *oraenv* command with a supplied parameter to set up the environment.

🖫 check_local_database_connection.sh

```
#!/bin/bash

# If a SID is provided as an argument it will be set and oraenv run
# otherwise we will use the current SID.  If no SID is set or
provided
# an error message is displayed and the script exits with a status
of 1
if [ $1 ]
then
    ORACLE_SID=$1
    ORAENV_ASK=NO
    . oraenv
else
    if [ ! $ORACLE_SID ]
    then
            echo "Error: No ORACLE_SID set or provided as an
argument"
            exit 1
    fi
fi

# A second parameter of a username/password can be provided or the
default
# given here can be used
if [ $2 ]
then
    user_pass=$2
else
    user_pass='scott/tiger'
fi
```

```
# Define the location of the temporary file this script will use
tempfile=/tmp/check_local_database_$ORACLE_SID.txt

# Start sqlplus and connect as the specified user
sqlplus -S $user_pass@$ORACLE_SID << EOF > $tempfile

    exit

EOF

# If the exit status of sqlplus was not 0 then we will send an email
if [ $? != 0 ]
then
    mail -s "Error connecting to $ORACLE_SID" oracle < $tempfile
fi

rm $tempfile
```

A second parameter can be used to specify the username and password to use. If these are not specified a default is used.

You may want to create an account with minimal privileges to use for connection tests like this and change the script to use your default. If you do this you will want to lock down the file permissions (*chmod 700 check_local_database.sh*) to assure that other users on the system cannot view the password, and of course you should never use scott/tiger as a username/password pair.

The *check_database_connection.sh* script below can be used to check a database which is on a separate system. Since there would be no entry in the local *oratab* file for a remote database, this script uses the current user's *.profile* to configure the Oracle environment, including the ORACLE_HOME and PATH variables.

💾 check_database_connection.sh

```
#!/bin/bash

# This script uses the user's .profile to set up the environmental
variables
# rather than oraenv since an oratab file may not exist for the
given database
```

```
. ~/.profile

# A second parameter of a username/password can be provided or the
default
# given here can be used
if [ $2 ]
then
    user_pass=$2
else
    user_pass='scott/tiger'
fi

# Define the location of the temporary file this script will use
tempfile=/tmp/check_database_connection_$ORACLE_SID.txt

# Start sqlplus and connect as the specified user
sqlplus -S $user_pass@$1 << EOF > $tempfile

    exit

EOF

# If the exit status of sqlplus was not 0 then we will send an email
if [ $? != 0 ]
then
    mail -s "Error connecting to $ORACLE_SID from `hostname`" oracle
< $tempfile
fi

rm $tempfile
```

It is preferable to use the *oraenv* script for local databases, but when connecting to databases on other systems this method will work assuming the .profile has been configured. This could be excluded altogether if the script were only to be used interactively, but when running scripts from a *crontab* entry the login scripts must be specified.

Like the *check_listener.sh* script this script can be run frequently to confirm database availability. The following crontab entry runs the *check_database_connection.sh* script every 15 minutes.

```
00,15,30,45 * * * *
/u01/app/oracle/admin/common/check_database_connection.sh oss
```

Monitor Free Space within Tablespaces

In chapter 12 we saw a script to display tablespace usage on demand. The following scripts can be set up in a crontab entry to automatically email the administrator on a regular basis, or only when a tablespace has filled up beyond a threshold.

The *tablespace_usage_report.sh* script uses the same output but redirected to a file. The file is then used as the body of an email to the oracle user. The partial listing of the script shows some of the key differences. The whole script can be viewed in the code depot.

> 💾 **tablespace_usage_report.sh (partial script shown)**

```
#!/bin/bash

...

# Here we enter SQL*Plus with the silent option, format the output
# and execute a query to check the tablespace usage
sqlplus -S "/ as sysdba" << EOF > $tempfile

...

EOF

mail -s "$ORACLE_SID Tablespace Usage" oracle < $tempfile

rm $tempfile
```

We see that a tempfile variable is used to define the file location where we will keep the output of the query. When the sqlplus command is called we redirect the output into this tempfile and later use it as the input for the *mail* command. Finally the script removes the tempfile after the mail has been sent.

Since this script will generate an email every time it is run it is probably best to run it on only a daily or weekly basis. Saving an archive of these emails can be useful for tracking long term space

---

usage trends. The following crontab entry would cause the script to be run every Monday morning at 5:00 am.

```
00 05 * * 1 /u01/app/oracle/admin/common/tablespace_usage_report.sh
oss
```

The *tablespace_usage_alert.sh* script is somewhat more sophisticated. It runs a similar query to the previous script; however, logic has been added to only show tablespaces which are above a certain threshold. The threshold is set to 85and can be easily altered.

⊟ tablespace_usage_alert.sh (partial script shown)

```
#!/bin/bash

# Set the percent above which the DBAs should be warned
threshold=85

...

# Here we enter SQL*Plus with the silent option, format the output
# and execute a query to check the tablespace usage
sqlplus -S "/ as sysdba" << EOF > $tempfile

set linesize 80
column percent_used format a12

define exit_status = 0

column xs new_value exit_status

select
    files.tablespace_name,
    files.size_in_mb,
    used.used_in_mb,
    round((used.used_in_mb/files.size_in_mb)*100) || '%' as
percent_used,
    1 as xs
from
    (
        select tablespace_name, round(sum(bytes)/1024/1024) as
size_in_mb
        from dba_data_files
        group by tablespace_name
    ) files,
    (
        select tablespace_name, round(sum(bytes)/1024/1024) as
used_in_mb
        from dba_extents
        group by tablespace_name
```

```
      ) used
where files.tablespace_name = used.tablespace_name
and 100*used.used_in_mb/files.size_in_mb > $threshold
order by tablespace_name;

exit &exit_status

EOF

# If the exit status of sqlplus was not 0 then we will send an email
if [ $? != 0 ]
then
    mail -s "WARNING: Low tablespace free in $ORACLE_SID" oracle <
$tempfile
fi

rm $tempfile
```

The variable threshold is a shell variable; however, since we are redirecting input into SQL*Plus we are able to use it inline in the where statement of the query. Within SQL*Plus we have also defined an *exit_status* variable and assigned it the value of 0. By selecting 1 into that variable (through the column xs) we know that *exit_status* will be set to 1 if any rows are selected, otherwise *exit_status* will remain 0.

By using the *exit_status* variable as an argument when exiting SQL*Plus we set the $? variable for the following *if* statement to read. If the exit status was set to something other than 0, we know there is a tablespace above the threshold.

On production systems, the DBAs will want to know as soon as possible when a tablespace is near full so it is probably good to have this script run frequently. The crontab below shows how this script could be run hourly at five minutes past each hour, but since this script only generates email when there is a problem you could even run it more frequently.

```
05 * * * * /u01/app/oracle/admin/common/tablespace_usage_alert.sh
oss
```

Table is Writeable, Readable or Other Specific SQL

The following script could be adapted to test any SQL statement. It will execute the statement and, in this case, rollback the results and exit. If a SQL error is generated on execution, SQL*Plus will exit with an error in the result code.

💾 test_sql.sh

```
#!/bin/bash

# If a SID is provided as an argument it will be set and oraenv run
# otherwise we will use the current SID.  If no SID is set or
provided
# an error message is displayed and the script exits with a status
of 1
if [ $1 ]
then
    ORACLE_SID=$1
    ORAENV_ASK=NO
    . oraenv
else
    if [ ! $ORACLE_SID ]
    then
            echo "Error: No ORACLE_SID set or provided as an
argument"
            exit 1
    fi
fi

# A second parameter of a username/password can be provided or the
default
# given here can be used
if [ $2 ]
then
    user_pass=$2
else
    user_pass='scott/tiger'
fi

# Define the location of the temporary file this script will use
tempfile=/tmp/test_sql_$ORACLE_SID.txt

# Start sqlplus and connect as the specified user
sqlplus -S $user_pass@$ORACLE_SID << EOF > $tempfile

    whenever sqlerror exit 1 rollback

    select empno from emp where empno=7902;
```

```
    insert into emp values(1000, 'Emmons', 'DBA', null, null, null,
null, null);

    rollback;

    exit;

EOF

# If the exit status of sqlplus was not 0 then we will send an email
if [ $? != 0 ]
then
    mail -s "SQL error in $ORACLE_SID" oracle < $tempfile
fi

rm $tempfile
```

The statement *whenever sqlerror exit 1 rollback* changes the behavior of SQL*Plus. When it encounters an error instead of simply printing it in the output it will print the error, perform a rollback and exit SQL*Plus with a result code of 1. Like previous scripts the result code is used to determine if an email should be sent.

While this type of test seems like it should be unnecessary, if there is a recurring problem with a table, procedure, constraint or other database object, a script like this one can help improve the speed at which you can identify and respond to a problem.

As with other scripts of this type you will want to be careful of file permissions. Removing all permissions for the group and other users is typically the best course of action.

The frequency at which you run this script will be highly dependant on what it is checking and the desired response time in case of a problem. Since it rolls back the changes the script will not generate a large amount of data even if it is run frequently.

Check for Invalid Objects

When a user or script tries to use an object which has been marked as 'invalid' Oracle will try to recompile it on the fly and make it ready to serve the request. This usually works, but can be time consuming, causing a delay in servicing a user's request. To reduce the likelihood of this delay and to regularly scan for invalid objects (which may be a sign that something bad is happening) the *check_for_invalid_objects.sh* script will check the *dba_objects* table for invalid objects and if any are found it will kick off the Oracle delivered *utlrp.sql* script to recompile invalid objects.

🖫 check_for_invalid_objects.sh

```
#!/bin/bash

# If a SID is provided as an argument it will be set and oraenv run
# otherwise we will use the current SID.  If no SID is set or
provided
# an error message is displayed and the script exits with a status
of 1
if [ $1 ]
then
    ORACLE_SID=$1
    ORAENV_ASK=NO
    . oraenv
else
    if [ ! $ORACLE_SID ]
    then
        echo "Error: No ORACLE_SID set or provided as an
argument"
        exit 1
    fi
fi

# Define the location of the temporary file this script will use
tempfile=/tmp/check_for_invalid_objects_$ORACLE_SID.txt

# Start sqlplus and connect as sysdba
sqlplus -S "/ as sysdba" << EOF1 > /dev/null

    define exit_status = 0

    column xs new_value exit_status

    select 1 as xs from dba_objects where status!='VALID';
```

```
     exit &exit_status

EOF1

# If the exit status of sqlplus was not 0 then we will lauch sqlplus
# to run utlrp.sql and send an email
if [ $? != 0 ]
then

     sqlplus -S "/ as sysdba" << EOF2 > $tempfile

          set pagesize

          select count(*) || ' invalid objects found.  Running
utlrp.'
          from dba_objects where status!='VALID';

          set pagesize 32

          @?/rdbms/admin/utlrp.sql

EOF2

     mail -s "Invalid objects found in $ORACLE_SID" oracle <
$tempfile

fi

rm $tempfile
```

This script uses the exit status from SQL*Plus to determine if we should launch SQL*Plus again to recompile invalid objects. This logic could have been handled with dynamic SQL or PL/SQL but this is a shell scripting book, not a SQL book. The added overhead of launching SQL*Plus a second time is negligible.

Both times SQL*Plus is called, it uses file markers to take commands directly from the shell script. Notice that different file markers are used for each. It is essential that if you use file markers more than once within a script that each set of file markers is unique.

We also see that, although the second call to SQL*Plus is indented by one tab, the ending file marker is at the beginning of the line. The shell looks for the ending file marker to be at the beginning of a line so it cannot be indented.

Checking for invalid objects should not have to be done frequently unless active development is being done on a database. In most cases it should suffice to run the *check_for_invalid_objects.sh* script a few times a day. The following crontab entry will run the script at 30 minutes past 1 am, 7 am, 1 pm and 7 pm.

```
30 1,7,13,19 * * *
/u01/app/oracle/admin/common/check_for_invalid_objects.sh oss
```

Conclusion

There are simply a ton of things that could be useful to monitor within a database and each database will need a different set of things monitored. While the scripts given here are just the tip of the iceberg they can all be easily adapted to your exact needs.

The listener is the gateway to your database. We saw how the *lsnrctl***Error! Bookmark not defined.** command can be used to check the status of the listener and how a script can then restart it if necessary.

Two scripts were given which can be used to check if a valid SQL connection can be made to a database. One script will check on a database on the local system and the other which can be used to check a remote database. Neither of these scripts will attempt to restart a downed database but rather will notify the administrator so they can determine the cause of the problem before restarting.

While Oracle provides functionality to automatically extend tablespaces, it is useful to monitor tablespace usage and extend them manually when possible. This will prevent the user experiencing a delay while the tablespace extends.

The *test_sql.sh* script could be adapted to run almost any SQL commands and will send an email if any of them generate SQL errors. The email will contain the details of the transaction indicating what statement caused the error.

Checking for invalid objects within the database can also help prevent users from experiencing a delay. If objects are invalid, the *check_for_invalid_objects.sh* script will not only notify the administrator, but will also kick off Oracle's *utlrp.sql* script to recompile them.

Even though some of these scripts will automatically correct a problem they still notify the administrator. This allows the administrator to remain aware of the health of the database. If something is frequently invalidating objects or the listener is crashing a lot, the administrator should know to look for and correct the root cause of these problems even though they could just allow the script to continue correcting the problem.

In the next chapter, we will look at some scripts to maintain and monitor Oracle Application Servers.

Oracle Application Server

Oracle Application Server (OAS) is a completely different product from Oracle Database, but the two products are so integrated that Application Server maintenance typically resides with the DBA.

The scripts in this chapter are designed to handle basic, stand-alone Oracle Application Servers. More complex infrastructures, including those that rely on a metadata repository, could be managed through a combination of these scripts and database maintenance scripts.

Starting and Stopping Oracle Application Server

There are two primary commands which are used to start Oracle Application Server, *dcmctl* which starts the distributed configuration manager and *opmnctl* which starts the Oracle Process Manager and Notification Server which subsequently starts the web server and other configured servers. In some versions of OAS the *dcmctl* command will start the *opmn* process as well. This script will start each separately but if *dcmctl* does start *opmn* there there is no harm in running the *opmn* command again.

start_oas.sh

```
#!/bin/bash

ORACLE_HOME=/u01/app/oracle/product/as_10.1.2
export ORACLE_HOME
```

```
# Define the location of the temporary file this script will use
tempfile=/tmp/start_oas.txt

# Set the result_code variable to 0
result_code=0

# Start the distributed configuration management
$ORACLE_HOME/dcm/bin/dcmctl start > $tempfile

if [ $? != 0 ]
then
    result_code=1
fi

# Start the Oracle Process Manager
$ORACLE_HOME/opmn/bin/opmnctl startall >> $tempfile

if [ $? != 0 ]
then
    result_code=1
fi

# If the exit status for any of the above commands was non-zero send
an email
if [ result_code != 0 ]
then
    mail -s "Problem starting OAS on `hostname`" oracle < $tempfile
fi

rm $tempfile
```

This script manually sets the ORACLE_HOME variable for the application server. You will need to update this variable with the location of OAS on your system.

The script runs several commands and we are concerned about the result code for each. The *result_code* variable is set to 0 at the beginning of the script and if either of the commands fail the following *if* statement will change the value of *result_code* to 1. This then indicates that an email notification should be sent.

The corresponding *stop_oas.sh* script is almost identical except it will stop OPMN before stopping DCM.

```
#!/bin/bash

ORACLE_HOME=/u01/app/oracle/product/as_10.1.2
export ORACLE_HOME

# Define the location of the temporary file this script will use
tempfile=/tmp/start_oas.txt

# Set the result_code variable to 0
result_code=0

# Stop the Oracle Process Manager
$ORACLE_HOME/opmn/bin/opmnctl stopall >> $tempfile

if [ $? != 0 ]
then
     result_code=1
fi

# Stop the distributed configuration management
$ORACLE_HOME/dcm/bin/dcmctl shutdown > $tempfile

if [ $? != 0 ]
then
     result_code=1
fi

# If the exit status for any of the above commands was non-zero send
an email
if [ result_code != 0 ]
then
     mail -s "Problem shutting down OAS on `hostname`" oracle <
$tempfile
fi

rm $tempfile
```

These scripts could be called at system startup or shutdown to cleanly start and stop OAS. Each platform handles startup and shutdown differently so you will have to work with your system administrator to set this up.

Cleaning Up Web Server Log Files

There are several log files associated with an Oracle Application Server but few of them grow very quickly. Depending on your configuration you may have to rotate them manually (using a method like the *rotate_alert_logs.sh* script presented in chapter 12) but recent versions of OAS automatically rotate the most active logs: the *access_log* and *error_log* for the web server.

OAS appends a timestamp to these logs continually creating logs with filenames like *access_log.1173441600*. Over time, hundreds or thousands of these logs can build up. Depending on your sites requirements it is typically safe to keep only newer logs around.

The *remove_old_http_logs.sh* script will remove logs older than a certain number of days. The number of days to keep is controlled by the *days_to_keep* variable.

💾 remove_old_http_logs.sh

```
#!/bin/bash

ORACLE_HOME=/u01/app/oracle/product/as_10.1.2

days_to_keep=30

find $ORACLE_HOME/Apache/Apache/logs -name "access_log.*" \
-mtime +$days_to_keep -exec rm {} \;

find $ORACLE_HOME/Apache/Apache/logs -name "error_log.*" \
-mtime +$days_to_keep -exec rm {} \;
```

The *-name* option to the *find* command assures that we will only remove files which match the pattern "access_log.*" and the *-mtime* option tells the script to only remove files which are more than the specified number of days old. By using several options of the *find* command, we can specify exactly which files we wish to remove without the danger of this script removing any necessary files.

For most sites it will be sufficient to run this script daily. The crontab entry below will run this script every morning at 1:00.

```
00 01 * * * /u01/app/oracle/admin/common/remove_old_http_logs.sh
```

Starting and Stopping the Application Server Console

The web console for Oracle Application Server allows the administrator to manage several aspects of the OAS instance through an easy to use web interface. The console is not automatically started when OAS starts up and you may not wish to leave it running as it consumes some resources and is not used on a daily basis after initial setup.

Only one command is needed to start the application server console so in this case a shell script is probably overkill. Instead this function is a good candidate for an alias.

The following lines show the syntax for configuring an alias. To make these aliases available every time you log into a system, you can add them to your *.profile* file.

Add the following lines to your .profile to use these aliases

```
alias start_console='emctl start iasconsole'
alias stop_console='emctl stop iasconsole'
```

Once configured, all you need to do to use the alias is type *start_console* or *stop_console*. The output of the commands will be printed directly to the screen.

Check Running OPMN Processes

The Oracle Process Manager and Notification command is used to manage a number of separate processes, most notably the HTTP server and the Oracle Container for Java (OC4J). Using the *opmnctl* command, the *check_opmn_processes.sh* script can be used to check the status of processes controlled by OPMN and restart them if they are not alive.

This is one of the most complex scripts in this book. It will accept multiple process names arguments and process them one by one. This eliminates the need to run the script for each process you wish to monitor. The script also does more sophisticated testing of input and commands used than other scripts thus far.

💾 check_opmn_processes.sh

```
#!/bin/bash

ORACLE_HOME=/u01/app/oracle/product/as_10.1.2
export ORACLE_HOME

# If no arguments are specified
if [ ! $1 ]
then
    echo "Please specify one or more OPMN managed process to check"
    echo "example: 'check_process_status.sh HTTP_Server OC4J'"
    exit
fi

# This checks to see if the opmnctl command will run successfully
$ORACLE_HOME/opmn/bin/opmnctl status >/dev/null
if [ $? != 0 ]
then
    echo "Problem running opmnctl command, opmn may be down or
unavailable"
    exit
fi

# Define the location of the temporary file this script will use
tempfile=/tmp/check_process_status.txt

# One or more processes are given as arguments but they must be ones
# controlled by opmnctl such as HTTP_Server, OC4J, etc.
while [ "$*" != "" ]
do
    check_process=$1

    # Set the variable status by running opmnctl, using grep to find
the
    # appropriate line and cut to get the right column
    status=`$ORACLE_HOME/opmn/bin/opmnctl status | grep
$check_process \
    | cut -f4 -d'|'`

    # If status is blank that indicates that the given process was
not found
    # so the script prints an error and breaks out of the loop
```

```
        if [ "$status" = "" ]
        then
                echo "Process $check_process does not appear to be
managed by opmn"
                break
        fi

        # If the status is not Alive then call opmnctl to start the
process
        if [ ! $status = 'Alive' ]
        then
                $ORACLE_HOME/opmn/bin/opmnctl startproc \
                ias-component=$check_process > $tempfile
                result_code=$?
        fi

        # If the process did not come back as Alive then send an email
        # the result code from starting the process will determine the
subject
        if [ ! $status = 'Alive' ]
        then
                if [ "$result_code" = 0 ]
                then
                        mail -s "OAS process $check_process restarted on
`hostname`" \
                        oracle < $tempfile
                else
                        mail -s "OAS process $check_process problem
restarting on `hostname`" \
                        oracle < $tempfile
                fi
                rm $tempfile
        fi

        # Shift causes $1 to be discarded, $2 to become $1, $3 to become
$2
        # and so on allowing us to parse through the arguments
        shift
done
```

The script starts by confirming that at least one argument has been supplied and making sure the *opmnctl* command is available and working properly. If either of these conditions fails, the script will print an error to the screen and exit.

The majority of this script happens within a *while* loop which will repeat as long as there are parameters left to process. Only the first parameter ($1) is used each time through the loop. At the end of each time through the loop the *shift* command discards the first parameter and moves the value of each remaining parameter down one. When all parameters have been processed, the while condition will fail and the script is complete. This is an efficient way of iterating through arguments as long as you do not need to reuse them again later in the script. Otherwise, you would want to use a counter variable instead.

Within the script we see the *opmnctl* command being called and its output being manipulated to obtain a specific process' status. First *grep* is used to eliminate all lines except the one with the process on it, then *cut* is used to get only the status column. The result is put into the status variable which is used to determine what actions should be taken.

As with other scripts we send an email if the process is found to not be alive. The success or failure of restarting the process will determine the subject of the email.

You might want to run this script hourly to check OPMN processes. Running it more frequently is probably not necessary unless you are having a problem with managed processes.

```
00 01 * * * /u01/app/oracle/admin/common/check_opmn_processes.sh
HTTP_Server OC4J
```

Conclusion

Oracle Application Server maintenance is often a small part of the DBAs duties. With this in mind, it is nice to automate as much as possible reducing the need to memorize rarely used syntax.

OAS can be started and stopped automatically at system startup and shutdown. The scripts given here can also be used if there is a need to control OAS manually.

The web log files often continue to grow until there is a disk space issue. Continually maintaining the logs will reduce disk space usage as well as making backups of the system smaller.

Starting and stopping the Application Server Console is fairly simple but can be simplified even more through the use of a couple of aliases. Having aliases like this help eliminate the need to remember rarely used syntax.

The OPMN process is a fairly sophisticated utility which can be used to manage Oracle processes. A script was given which will check for a running process and start it if it is not alive.

The next chapter will show scripts for maintaining and monitoring at the operating system level. Proper maintenance and tuning of the operating system is essential for Oracle performance and stability.

Monitoring the System

It has been said enough to be almost cliché, but Oracle does not run in a vacuum. Factors like network performance, system load and disk space will kill the performance and availability of even the best tuned Oracle system. The scripts in this chapter will help maintain and monitor the system to help keep Oracle up and available.

Checking the System Log

There are several logs in the /var/log directory which contain information about specific services. The messages log is generally where information about the system is kept, making it of particular interest.

This script will email the system log to a list of users. Notice the list of users may contain users on the current system or email addresses on other systems.

🖫 send_messages_log.sh

```
#!/bin/bash

# Email addresses are listed here separated by commas
mail_to='root, oracle, jon@lifeaftercoffee.com'

# To send a different log simply change the definition of this
variable
log=/var/log/messages

# Grab the length of the file
length=`wc -l /var/log/messages  | cut -f1 -d' '`

tempfile=/tmp/send_messages_log.txt
```

```
echo "Contents of $log on `hostname`
" > $tempfile

i=$length

# This will move the lines from the log into the tempfile in reverse
order
while [ $i -gt 0 ]
do
    head -$i $log | tail -1 >> $tempfile
    i=`expr $i - 1`
done

# Send the temp file to the specified addresses
mail -s "`hostname` log $log" "$mail_to" < $tempfile

rm $tempfile
```

Rather than just sending the log as-is, this script reverses the order of the log entries. That causes the log to be listed from newest to oldest so the most recent events can easily be found at the top of the message.

Many administrators review these logs daily for problems. The following crontab entry will run this script every morning at 7:00.

```
00 07 * * *
/u01/app/oracle/admin/common/scripts/send_messages_log.sh
```

This example shows the script in the same location we have been using for other scripts but you may want to choose a different location for system related scripts. This is a good idea if you are going to have the script executed by root.

By default, the messages file can only be read by root; however, if you wish to have another user run this script you could change the permissions of the messages log.

Monitoring disk space

Between auto extending tablespaces, archive logs, and server logs Oracle's appetite for disk space can seem insatiable. In order to reduce the likelihood of disk space problems it is handy to have a script regularly check the amount of free space available.

As with the script which checked tablespaces for free space, a threshold is set in a variable at the beginning of the script. If you want to be alerted at a different level you can either provide the new percentage as an argument or change this variable in the script.

The ability to specify a different percentage as an argument allows the script to be run on a different schedule for a different threshold. As you will see in the *cron* examples for this script, it can be used to notify daily if the usage is above one threshold and hourly if it is above another.

check_disk_space.sh

```
#!/bin/bash

# Set the percentage used at which you would like to be alerted
max=85

# Email addresses are listed here separated by commas
mail_to='root, oracle, jon@lifeaftercoffee.com'

tempfile=/tmp/check_disk_space.txt

alert=n

# Take each percentage from the df command and check it against the
defined max
# Some platforms may not require (or even recognize) the -P option
for df
for percent in `df -P | grep -v Filesystem |  awk '{ print $5 }' |
cut -d'%' -f1`
do
    if [ $percent -ge $max ]
    then
            alert=y
            break
```

```
     fi
done

# If a partition was above the threshold send a message with df
output
if [ ! $alert = 'n' ]
then
     df -k > $tempfile
     mail -s "Disk usage above $max% on `hostname`" $mail_to <
$tempfile
     rm $tempfile
fi
```

This script makes good use of the *for* loop in order to parse over
several lines of output. The output is first trimmed to just the
percentage of disk used by manipulating it with *grep*, *awk* and *cut*.

The *for* loop takes each resulting line, which now only contains a
number, and compares it with the max set at the beginning of the
script. As soon as one file system is found to be above the
maximum, the *alert* variable is set and we break out of the loop.

Finally, email is sent with an entire *df* report only if *alert* has been
altered from its initial value of 'n'. This script could be made to
email information only about file systems which are above the
threshold; however, in my opinion the additional complexity is
not justified. Emailing the complete *df* output may also help the
administrator determine what other file systems may be filling up
or where space may be available.

As mentioned in the comments of this script, the *df* command
has a *-P* option which may not be necessary or even work on
some platforms. The option causes the output of *df* to be limited
to one line per file system simplifying the processing in our script.
If this script generates an error like *df: invalid option -- P* then this
flag should be removed and the script should function properly.

Since disk can fill up quickly under certain circumstances it can
be useful to run this script quite frequently. The first crontab

entry below will run this at 45 minutes past the hour, every hour of the day. Keep in mind that you will receive an email from this script every time it runs until space is freed up to bring it below the threshold.

```
45 * * * * /u01/app/oracle/admin/common/scripts/check_disk_space.sh
15 7 * * 1-5
/u01/app/oracle/admin/common/scripts/check_disk_space.sh 75
```

The second crontab entry above specifies a different threshold as an argument. This entry will send an email at 7:15 am, Monday through Friday if the disk usage is above 75%. This can give administrators some advanced notice that disk is getting low, but is not yet critical.

Since the *df* command can generally be run by any user this script can also be used by any user on the system.

On many UNIX and UNIX-like operating systems there are file systems which we do not need to check and others still that we may want to check with different thresholds. The *check_filesystem_space.sh* script allows the user to specify exactly which file systems to check. In addition the user must specify the threshold at which they would like to be notified.

💾 check_filesystem_space.sh

```
#!/bin/bash

# Set the percentage used at which you would like to be alerted
# Use argument 1 if provided or use a given default.
if [ ! $2 ]
then
    echo "No filesystems specified."
    echo "Usage: check_filesystem_space.sh 90 / /u01"
    exit 1
fi

max=$1

# Email addresses are listed here separated by commas
mail_to='root, oracle, jon@lifeaftercoffee.com'
```

```
tempfile=/tmp/check_filesystem_space.txt

alert=n

# Take each percentage from the df command and check it against the
defined max
# Some platforms may not require (or even recognize) the -P option
for df
while [ $2 ]
do
    percent=`df -P $2 | tail -1 |  awk '{ print $5 }' | cut -d'%' -
f1`

    if [ $percent -ge $max ]
    then
            alert=y
            break
    fi

    shift

done

# If a partition was above the threshold send a message with df
output
if [ ! $alert = 'n' ]
then
    df -k > $tempfile
    mail -s "Disk usage above $max% on `hostname`" $mail_to <
$tempfile
    rm $tempfile
fi
```

This script is very similar to *check_disk_space.sh* but instead of performing a full *df* listing it employs the second argument to see which file system should be checked. Since the script only lists one file system at a time the *tail* command can be used to view only the last line of the output therefore excluding the column headers.

If the file system checked is above the specified threshold then the alert variable is set and the script breaks out of the loop. If not, the loop continues and the *shift* command is used to move on to the next argument, if present.

The flexibility of this script allows different file systems to be checked at different frequencies and thresholds. The following crontab entries check /u01, /u02 and /u03 every 15 minutes to make sure none of these exceeds 85%. The second entry checks the / partition (which typically changes much less often) hourly to make sure it does not exceed 90%.

```
00,15,30,45 * * * *
/u01/app/oracle/admin/common/scripts/check_filesystem_space.sh 85
/u01 /u02 /u03
20 * * * *
/u01/app/oracle/admin/common/scripts/check_filesystem_space.sh 90 /
```

By changing the hour range you could also adapt this script to check a file system for different thresholds at different times of day. For instance, if you have a /backup file system where Oracle backups are sent, the usage of this file system may spike every night when backups are performed. You certainly want to be alerted before the file system fills up, but a higher threshold may be appropriate during the backup window.

Assuming your backup window is between midnight and six a.m. the following crontab entries will alert you if usage on the /backup file system exceeds 90% during the backup window or 75% at any other time.

```
00,15,30,45 0-5 * * *
u01/app/oracle/admin/common/scripts/check_filesystem_space.sh 90
/backup
00,15,30,45 6-23 * * *
u01/app/oracle/admin/common/scripts/check_filesystem_space.sh 90
/backup
```

Find the Size of a Directory

When it comes time to free up some disk space it is very handy to be able to sum up the size of directories and their contents. The *du* command presented in chapter 4 can be used to sum up directories. The following alias changes the default behavior of *du* to cause it to show summary information in human readable format.

```
$ alias du='du -hs'
$ du *
3.1G    10.2.0
698M    as_10.1.2
```

This alias can be added to your *.profile* to automatically have it available with every session. If you want to temporarily change the default action you can type *unalias du* to revert it to its default behavior.

Monitoring system load

One of the best indications of overall system performance is the *load average*. The load average is most commonly seen as part of the output of the *uptime* command.

```
$ uptime
 12:32:56 up 30 days, 21:43,  4 users,  load average: 3.29, 3.62,
4.12
```

Here is a somewhat simplified explanation of what the load average indicates.

The load average indicates the average number of processes running or waiting to run over the indicated period of time. The output listed above indicates that in the last minute there has been an average of 3.29 processes running or waiting to run on this system.

The load average output does not indicate if the processes were running or waiting to run over the indicated time period, but it is a fair generalization to say that if the load average is less than the number of processors, the system is in general keeping up with its workload.

If the load average is higher than the number of processes there are likely processes waiting to run which may impact user performance. If the load average grows to several times the number of processes, you probably already have angry users.

The output gives us the 1, 5 and 15 minute load averages, therefore we can make some assumptions on the direction the load is headed. If the 1 minute load average is lower than the 5 and 15 minute the load can be said to be decreasing. If the 1 minute load average is higher than the 5 and 15 the load is likely increasing.

While there is more to it, this should serve as an operational understanding for most purposes. By monitoring the load average we can get an idea of general system health and possibly respond to problems before they impact users.

The *monitor_load_average.sh* script will check the 1, 5 and 15 minute load averages against defined thresholds. Each increment can have a different threshold value. Generally you will want a fairly high threshold for the 1 minute load average since a short spike in load will force this up quickly. The 5 and 15 minute load averages indicate a more prolonged load on the system and therefore should have a lower threshold.

Since there is some variation in the exact text of the *uptime* output you may need to change the *load_text* variable to match the output of your *uptime* command.

🖫 monitor_load_average.sh

```
#!/bin/bash

# Set threshold for 1, 5 and 15 minute load averages (whole numbers
only)
# configured for a 2-processor system
max_1=8
max_5=6
```

```
max_15=4

# Set the string which appears before the load average in the uptime
command
load_text='load average: '

# Email addresses are listed here separated by commas
mail_to='root, oracle, jon@lifeaftercoffee.com'

alert=n

up=`uptime`

# Parse out the current load averages from the uptime command
load_1=`echo $up | awk -F "$load_text" '{ print $2 }' | cut -d, -f1
| cut -d. -f1`

load_5=`echo $up | awk -F "$load_text" '{ print $2 }' | cut -d, -f2
| cut -d. -f1`

load_15=`echo $up | awk -F "$load_text" '{ print $2 }' | cut -d, -f3
| cut -d. -f1`

# Set alert=y if any of the averages are above their thresholds
if [ $load_1 -ge $max_1 ]
then
    alert=y
elif [ $load_5 -ge $max_5 ]
then
    alert=y
elif [ $load_15 -ge $max_15 ]
then
    alert=y
fi

# Send email if the alert variable was set
if [ ! $alert = n ]
then
    mail -s "High load on `hostname`" $mail_to < `uptime`
fi
```

Like the *check_disk_space.sh* script, the *monitor_load_average.sh* script uses a series of commands piped together to parse out the appropriate numbers for comparison. In this case, the load average is taken from the end of the *uptime* output and parsed down to a single integer, discarding everything past the whole number.

Each load average is then compared against its threshold and, if it has exceeded its threshold, the *alert* variable is set to 'y'. Mail is then sent based on the value of the *alert* variable.

This script should be run frequently to detect high load on the system, but running it more often than every 5 minutes is probably unnecessary. The following crontab entry will run *monitor_load_average.sh* every 5 minutes.

```
00,05,10,15,20,25,30,35,40,45,50,55 * * * *
/u01/app/oracle/admin/common/scripts/monitor_load_average.sh
```

Save Load Averages in Oracle

Historical data on the load average of the system can help identify when peak loads happen and is useful for long-term capacity planning. Few operating systems track any historical performance data by themselves; however, this script can be run in *cron* to regularly gather load information and store it in a table in an *oracle* database.

The *store_load_average.sh* script stores the 1, 5 and 15 minute load averages in a *load_average* table in the *os_stats* schema. The script *create_os_stats_schema.sql* is provided in the code depot to create this schema and table.

🖫 store_load_average.sh

```
#!/bin/bash

connect_string='os_stats/os_stats@oss'

. ~/.profile

# Since the database may be on a different machine we use the 'no
sid'
# option for oraenv to set the ORACLE_HOME variable
ORACLE_SID='*'
export ORACLE_SID

ORAENV_ASK=NO
```

```
. oraenv

tempfile=/tmp/store_load_average.txt

# Set the string which appears before the load average in the uptime
command
load_text='load average: '

up=`uptime`

# Parse out the current load averages from the uptime command
load_1=`echo $up | awk -F "$load_text" '{ print $2 }' | cut -d, -f1`

load_5=`echo $up | awk -F "$load_text" '{ print $2 }' | cut -d, -f2`

load_15=`echo $up | awk -F "$load_text" '{ print $2 }' | cut -d, -
f3`

# Connect through sqlplus and store the load averages into the
database
sqlplus -S $connect_string << EOF > $tempfile

    whenever sqlerror exit 1

    insert into load_average
            (hostname, load_date, load_1_minute, load_5_minute,
load_15_minute)
    values
            ('hostname', sysdate, $load_1, $load_5, $load_15);

    commit;

EOF

# Output some text if there was a problem
if [ ! $? = 0 ]
then
    echo "Problem with store_load_average.sh script"
    cat $tempfile
fi

rm $tempfile
```

The output of the *uptime* command is parsed out similarly to the
last script except in this case the decimal information is retained.
The *load_1*, *load_5*, and *load_15* variables are then used as input to
SQL*Plus to load their values, plus the hostname and date, into
the *load_average* table.

Since the *load_average* table includes a *hostname*, filed statistics for
multiple systems may be stored in a single database. Once in a

table, the load information can be easily retrieved and graphed with a utility like Oracle Discoverer.

In order to gather complete performance data on a system it would be best to run this script every minute. This may be overkill for some scenarios, but will assure the most data possible is collected. The following crontab will run every minute of every day to gather load information.

```
* * * * * /u01/app/oracle/admin/common/scripts/store_load_average.sh
```

Running this every minute will generate 1,440 entries per host every day. If you are monitoring just 6 hosts that can add up to over a million rows after just 4 months! This volume of data is not unreasonable for Oracle to handle, but the useful lifespan of the data should be considered and the table eventually trimmed.

The following script will trim old records out of the *load_average* table. I have set the script to keep records for 90 days, but 30 may be more reasonable in some environments.

🖫 load_average_cleanup.sh

```bash
#!/bin/bash

days_to_keep=90

connect_string='os_stats/os_stats@oss'

. ~/.profile


# Define the location of the temporary file this script will use
tempfile=/tmp/session_audit_cleanup_$ORACLE_SID.txt

# Since the database may be on a different machine we use the 'no
sid'
# option for oraenv to set the ORACLE_HOME variable
ORACLE_SID='*'
export ORACLE_SID

ORAENV_ASK=NO
. oraenv
```

```
tempfile=/tmp/load_average_cleanup.txt

# Start sqlplus and check for locked accounts
sqlplus -S $connect_string << EOF > $tempfile

    whenever sqlerror exit 1

    delete from load_average where load_date < sysdate -
$days_to_keep;

    commit;

    exit;

EOF

# Output an error if there was a problem
if [ $? = 0 ]
then
    echo "Problem cleaning load_average in $ORACLE_SID"
    cat $tempfile
fi

rm $tempfile
```

It is probably not necessary to run the cleanup script more than once a week. This crontab entry will clean up the table every Sunday morning at 6:15 am. This will keep the *load_average* table from growing indefinitely.

```
45 06 * * 0
/u01/app/oracle/admin/common/scripts/load_average_cleanup.sh
```

Gathering CPU Usage Statistics from sar

There is an almost infinite list of utilities which can be used to monitor different aspects of a UNIX system. One long time favorite is the *sar* utility. *sar* may not be installed on your system by default; however, it is available for most popular UNIX and Linux distributions.

The *sa1* command is run by root, typically from a crontab entry like the one below. *sa1* collects data about the system which can

then be displayed using the *sar* command. This example gathers
system data every 10 minutes.

```
00,10,20,30,40,50 * * * * /usr/lib/sa/sa1 1 1
```

The *sa1* command collects a large amount of information about
the system that can then be displayed by the *sar* command. By
default, the *sar* command will display information about CPU
usage and the following script will capture that data and store it in
a table in a database. The script *create_cpu_usage_table.sh* will create
the table in which to store this information.

store_cpu_usage.sh

```bash
#!/bin/bash

# Check for arguments and set variables appropriately
if [ ! $# = 0 ]
then
    if [ ! $# = 2 ]
    then
            echo "To load a file from another day provide the file
location"
            echo "and the date of the file in MM/DD/YYYY format"
            echo "example: store_cpu_usage.sh /var/log/sa/sa21
03/21/2007"
            exit
    fi
    sar_command="sar -f $1"
    load_date=$2
else
    sar_command="sar"
    load_date=`date '+%m/%d/%y'`
fi

sql_file=/tmp/store_cpu_usage.sql

logfile=/tmp/store_cpu_usage.txt

# Update this with your connect information
connect_string='os_stats/os_stats@oss'

# Define how many lines of header must be skipped
skip_lines=3

. ~/.profile

# Since the database may be on a different machine we use the 'no
sid'
```

```
# option for oraenv to set the ORACLE_HOME variable
ORACLE_SID='*'
export ORACLE_SID

ORAENV_ASK=NO
. oraenv

# Remove any old sql file
if [ -f $sql_file ]
then
     rm $sql_file
fi

line_count=0

# Run the sar command and redirect its output into a while loop
$sar_command | while read line
do
     line_count=`expr $line_count + 1`
     if [ $line_count -gt $skip_lines ]
     then
             load_time=`echo $line | cut -f1 -d' '`
             if [ ! $load_time = "Average:" ]
             then
                     am_pm=`echo $line | cut -f2 -d' '`
                     cpu_user=`echo $line | cut -f4 -d' '`
                     cpu_nice=`echo $line | cut -f5 -d' '`
                     cpu_system=`echo $line | cut -f6 -d' '`
                     cpu_iowait=`echo $line | cut -f7 -d' '`
                     cpu_idle=`echo $line | cut -f8 -d' '`
# Generate the SQL to insert the records
                     sql="insert into cpu_usage
(hostname, sample_date, cpu_user, cpu_nice,
cpu_system, cpu_iowait, cpu_idle)
values
('`hostname`',
to_date('$load_date $load_time $am_pm', 'MM/DD/YYYY HH:MI:SS AM'),
$cpu_user, $cpu_nice, $cpu_system, $cpu_iowait, $cpu_idle);"
# Put the sql to insert the current line into the sql file
                     echo "$sql" >> $sql_file
             fi
     fi
done

# Finish off the
echo "commit;" >> $sql_file
echo "exit" >> $sql_file

# Connect through sqlplus and store the load averages into the
database
sqlplus -S $connect_string @$sql_file >> $logfile

# Check for ORA- errors in the logfile and output the file if found
grep 'ORA-' $logfile >/dev/null
if [ $? = 0 ]
then
```

```
      cat $logfile
fi

rm $sql_file
rm $logfile
```

There is a lot going on in this script but the meat of it is the *while loop* which employs the *read* command to parse each line of the *sar* command one at a time. Like other scripts the *cut* command is used to zero in on the exact element we are looking for. The individual elements are then used to create a SQL statement which is added to the SQL script file. Finally *sqlplus* is called to run the generated *sql* script to insert the data into the database.

By default *sar* will show today's data, therefore the script should be run last thing in the day. The following crontab entry will load the *sar* output at 11:55 each night.

```
55 23 * * * /u01/app/oracle/admin/common/store_cpu_usage.sh
```

If a load is missed or if you want to load a *sar* file from a previous day, the script will also take a file name as an argument but the date of the file must also be specified.

```
$ ./store_cpu_usage.sh /var/log/sa/sa20 03/20/2007
```

Like the *store_load_average.sh* script the *store_cpu_usage.sh* script will include a hostname with each record so multiple hosts can store their CPU data in the same table.

sar can retrieve many other statistics from your system. The man page will give you more ideas for information you could be gathering.

Synchronize a Directory on Several Systems

If you are using a common directory structure on all your systems (which I highly recommend), then you may find that you want to synchronize certain files and directories between systems. This can allow you to make a change in one place, and then easily propagate the change out to other systems.

This script will synchronize the contents of the directory */u01/app/oracle/admin/common/* to the systems specified in the *targets* variable.

🖫 copy_common_dir.sh

```
#!/bin/bash

# Define the systems that files should be copied to
targets="sprog
splunge
mernimbler"

# Define what directory you want to synchronize
directory='/u01/app/oracle/admin/common'

# Define any sub-directories or files which should be excluded from
the copy
# This line can be commented if there are no exclusions
exclude='--exclude logs'

# Synchronize the directory on each target
for target in $targets
do

    rsync -a $exclude --delete $directory $target:$directory

done
```

This very simple script can quickly synchronize a directory on a long list of hosts, especially if key authentication has been configured to eliminate the need for entering passwords. If key authentication has not been configured, you will simply be prompted to enter the password for each system.

This script is designed to be run interactively, and as such does not suppress or capture the output of commands run. It could be easily modified for running in a crontab by redirecting the output of *rsync* to a tempfile and checking the result code after each *rsync* execution.

Conclusion

Monitoring the system on which Oracle is running is important to maintaining a good running database. Shell scripting is the perfect tool for monitoring UNIX and Linux systems.

Checking the system logs is something which should be done regularly by the system administrator. A script was given to simplify this process by emailing a list of users the contents of the system logs. It even reorders the log into reverse chronological order so the most recent events appear at the beginning of the message.

The monitoring of free disk space is also important. A short but elegant script was given to check disk space usage and notify a list of users if a threshold is reached.

Of course once you know disk usage is high, you then have to do something about it. The *du* command was presented with a useful alias which will change the default behavior of *du*.

The system load average can give a good indication of overall system health. Two scripts were introduced on this topic: one to alert administrators if the load is above a certain threshold and another to store the load average information in an Oracle table for future analysis.

CPU usage can also be used to help identify bottlenecks in the system. We saw a script which uses the *sa1* command to gather statistics through the day and then employs the *sar* command to load them into a database.

Since we often have script directories and configuration files which we want to be identical on several systems we saw a script that employs *rsync* to synchronize a directory across a list of systems. The script can easily be adapted to work on a different directory simply by changing a couple variables.

In the final chapter we will take a look at how we can make use of shell scripting on Windows systems. While the tools and syntax are different on Windows, all the same principles apply.

Windows Scripting

While the major thrust of this book has obviously been shell scripting on UNIX and UNIX-like operating systems, many of the same tasks can be scripted on the Windows operating system. In this chapter we will examine some DOS scripts and have the opportunity to compare and contrast them with the UNIX scripts with which we have been working.

Windows scripts can be edited directly with a text editor just like UNIX scripts. Notepad or EditPlus are probably the best choices, but any editor that will save in a text-only format (no markup or formatting) can be used. Scripts should be saved with a *.bat* extension and Windows will automatically recognize these as shell scripts.

What's Different in Windows?

There are many obvious differences between UNIX scripting and Windows scripting. Most of these are just syntactical and, as we will see in the scripts in this chapter, Windows scripts are very similar to UNIX scripts. In order to ease the transition from UNIX to Windows here is a list of the major differences you will encounter.

- There is no she-bang (#!). Since the MS-DOS shell will always be used, there is no need to specify an interpreter in the script.

- Paths will contain backslashes (\) between directories rather than slashes (/).

- Absolute paths will begin with a drive letter like C: or D: to indicate what drive the data is on.

- File and directory names are not case sensitive.

- Variables are typically enclosed between percent signs (%) instead of being indicated by a dollar sign($).

- Variables are defined using the *set* command.

The examples in this chapter are not meant to be an exhaustive list; however, they should be enough to demonstrate how Windows scripts differ.

Database Exports

This Windows database export script is very similar to its UNIX counterpart. It expects arguments for username, password, SID and has additional variables set to handle other export options. If the proper number of arguments are not specified the script will display usage information.

🖫 full_export.bat

```
@echo off

if (%1%)==() goto USAGE
if (%2%)==() goto USAGE
if (%3%)==() goto USAGE
if (%4%)==() goto USAGE

set USERNAME=%1%
set PASSWORD=%2%
set SID=%3%
set FILE=%4%

set EXPARGUMENTS=BUFFER=10485760 FULL=Y

del /q %FILE%

exp USERID=%USERNAME%/%PASSWORD%@%SID% FILE=%FILE% LOG=%FILE%.log
%EXPARGUMENTS%

echo Export complete.  Check %FILE%.log for details

goto END
```

```
:USAGE
echo Usage: dba_full_export.bat username password SID
C:\path\to\file
goto END

:END
@echo on
```

Many differences between UNIX and Windows shell scripts are immediately obvious. Since there is (by default) only one shell interpreter on Windows there is no need for a *#!* line to indicate which shell to use.

The *@echo off* line suppresses the prompt from being displayed between each command. This helps to limit the amount of output sent to the screen while the script runs.

Retrieving the contents of an argument is accomplished by enclosing it in percent signs (%) rather than the leading dollar sign we have been using. Conventionally variables are noted in all caps; however, variables, commands, file names and other syntax are not case sensitive in Windows.

A simple *if* statement is used in this script to check if the right number of arguments has been passed to this script. If any of the arguments (represented by %1%, %2%, %3% and %4%) were not specified the script performs a *goto USAGE* which will cause the interpreter to look for the marker *:USAGE* and continue the script from that point.

Additional variables are set using the *set* command including copying the contents of the argument variables to more meaningful variable names. Note that there is no need to quote strings when setting variables.

Database Exports

The *del* command is used to remove the backup file if it exists. The quiet option is set with the */q* flag (instead of a dash (-)) since Windows uses a slash (/) to indicate options.

The *exp* command is run very similarly to how it was in our UNIX scripts using variables to fill in the appropriate arguments. Once run the *echo* command (which works surprisingly similar to its UNIX counterpart) is used to give some feedback on where the log file is kept.

A final *goto* statement allows us to skip the *:USAGE* portion of this script so we do not echo the usage to the user. As a final step *echo* is turned back on so, if run interactively, the shell will display the prompt for the user.

To run this script, simply call the script name with the appropriate arguments. Unlike in UNIX, no special permissions need to be set up on a *.bat* file to be able to execute it.

```
>dba_full_export.bat system manager ossw
C:\oracle_backups\ossw_full_export.dmp
```

RMAN backups

This RMAN backup script works a bit differently from its UNIX counterpart in that it uses RMAN command files to execute the actual RMAN commands. It allows the flexibility to use the same script with any database and any RMAN command file.

🖫   rman_backup.bat

```
@echo off

if (%1%)==() goto USAGE
if (%2%)==() goto USAGE
if (%3%)==() goto USAGE
if (%4%)==() goto USAGE

set USERNAME=%1%
```

```
set PASSWORD=%2%
set SID=%3%
set COMMAND_FILE=%4%

echo Starting RMAN backup

rman TARGET=%USERNAME%/%PASSWORD%@%SID% CMDFILE=%COMMAND_FILE%

echo Backup complete.

goto END

:USAGE
echo Usage: rman_backup.bat username password SID command_file
goto END

:END
@echo on
```

The script has many of the same elements of the export script with one major difference. The fourth argument is used to indicate which RMAN command file should be used. The following is an example of a simple RMAN command file which could be used with this script.

🖫 level_0_backup.rman

```
backup incremental level=0 database plus archivelog delete input;
delete noprompt obsolete;
quit;
```

I have chosen to name my backup files with the extension *.rman* in order to make it clear what the file is for. If your database uses an RMAN catalog you could add the catalog connection information into the *rman_backup.bat* script if it is used for all databases or only into the appropriate *.rman* command files if it should only be used with some backups.

Running a SQL Script

This simple shell script can make running a SQL script push-button simple. This is a great script for running reports or periodic checks on an Oracle system.

```
@echo off

REM Set the variables below with your connection and script
information
REM All output from sqlplus will be sent to the output file
set USERNAME=scott
set PASSWORD=tiger
set SID=ossw
set SQL_SCRIPT=D:\oracle\product\10.1.0\admin\common\report.sql
set
OUTPUT_FILE=D:\oracle\product\10.1.0\admin\common\logs\report.txt

REM run sqlplus in silent mode with the parameters set above
sqlplus -S %USERNAME%/%PASSWORD%@%SID% @%SQL_SCRIPT% > %OUTPUT_FILE%

@echo on
```

This script shows how the familiar method of redirecting command output to a file also works within Windows scripts.

By setting all the required information in variables, this script completely eliminates the need for user input. This is also useful for running scheduled jobs which cannot take user input or even arguments.

Other Scripting Options for Windows

Command line scripts in Windows are handy but offer far less flexibility than UNIX shell scripting. Several options are available for more advanced scripting, the most notable of which is Microsoft Visual Basic.

Programming in Visual Basic is more complicated than shell scripting and is beyond the scope of this book; but, if you are looking to do very sophisticated programming with error checking and intelligent decision making this may be the best route on Windows. The power of Visual Basic does come with the price of complexity and it can be much more difficult to get started.

Another option for scripting on Windows is to install a Linux-like framework like *Cygwin* (cygwin.com.) Cygwin is comprised of a DLL which emulates many of the resources available on Linux and a collection of familiar Linux commands.

Once installed, you can invoke the *Cygwin* application and you will be presented with a UNIX-like shell. From that shell you can browse your Windows file systems, manipulate files and directories, and even run scripts just like on a Linux system.

Most common UNIX and Linux commands are available within the *Cygwin* framework so many shell scripts will run within it with no alteration. If *Cygwin* is missing a command you wish to use it may be available for download from their site.

Scheduling Scripts in Windows

Where UNIX uses the *cron* command, Windows has a more user-friendly job scheduler. The Windows job scheduler can be found in the Control Panel folder under *Scheduled Tasks*. A new task can be scheduled by choosing the Add Scheduled Task. Once a task is scheduled it will show up in the *Scheduled Tasks* folder. Selecting the task will allow you to edit it and right clicking on it will allow you to delete it.

When you are scheduling a new task, the *Scheduled Task Wizard* will walk you through several steps where you can choose how often you would like the task to run, what time and with what privileges.

Figure 17.1: *The Windows Task Wizard*

The *Scheduled Task Wizard* allows for the periodic running of tasks on a daily, weekly or monthly basis. It also allows for control over one-time only tasks, tasks to run at startup, and tasks to run at login. Because of these added options, the Windows task scheduler takes place of both *cron* and *at* as well as offers some of the functionality we have seen in the *.profile*.

The *Scheduled Task Wizard* has several screens which allow you to choose the application or script to be run, the frequency, time of day and the user credentials which should be used for running the task. Several advanced options are also available including the ability to limit the run time of a job.

As of the time of this writing, Windows Scheduled Tasks do not provide any direct feedback on the success or failure of scheduled tasks. This is a very major and somewhat frightening oversight.

Because of this, it is very important that you examine any logs created and check the results of the scheduled tasks frequently.

Conclusion

For very basic scripts, Windows shell scripting is not much different than UNIX shell scripting. Commands, variables, options and arguments all work in much the same way with some syntactical differences.

A database export script showed that a simple yet flexible script can be easily achieved using only the basic elements of the Windows shell script. As in our UNIX backup script, this backup script uses several arguments to control the behavior of *exp*.

An *RMAN* backup script offers a somewhat different approach than we have seen by using a command file to execute the commands within RMAN. This allows for good flexibility with minimal complexity.

Sometimes all you need to do is run a SQL script. The *run_report.bat* script allows a SQL script to be called and the output to be sent to a file without any interaction with the user. This can be very useful for allowing users who are unfamiliar with SQL*Plus to execute SQL scripts at their convenience.

For more advanced scripting on Windows, Microsoft's Visual Basic offers a solid development environment but demands a higher level of programming ability than shell scripting.

Cygwin may offer a solution for some scripting needs on Windows. This collection of free, open-source tools provides a Linux-like environment and many essential tools on the Windows platform.

Windows *Scheduled Tasks* can be used to easily control repeating tasks. This offers much of the functionality of *cron* but does not include any type of automatic notification of output or script failure.

Book Summary

Shell scripting is a broad subject. By now you should feel that you have a good grasp on the main areas of shell scripting and how it can be applied in an Oracle environment.

Customizing your environment is a way to make yourself at home on a system. If something about the system bothers you, these methods will help you improve your working environment.

While there are thousands of tools available in Linux and UNIX we reviewed several of the most popular and useful ones. If you need a tool to do something more specific there is probably one out there, but I think you will find that most common tasks can be accomplished by creatively combining the tools presented in this book.

Writing shell scripts can be very simple or quite complex depending on the sophistication of the scripts. Through a few key techniques, SQL*Plus can easily be controlled through shell scripts allowing us to examine or manipulate a database.

The scripts presented demonstrate many common tasks. While the bulk of them pertain to Oracle Database scripts to interface with Oracle Application Server and system administration scripts were also given.

Shell scripting can be adapted to fulfill many different purposes. The scripts given in this book are just a starting point. As you identify needs in your environment consider how you can customize existing scripts to fulfill new needs.

Index

X

About the Author

Jon Emmons has been working with Oracle on Linux and UNIX systems for several years. Currently employed as a Senior Oracle Consultant, Jon has experience in both corporate and higher education. Jon has managed implementations ranging from desktop workstations for academic research to large multi-tier load balanced custom web application farms.

Shortly after college, Jon's command of system administration identified him as a good candidate for database administration. Since then he has worked extensively with Oracle database and application server on UNIX and Linux.

Jon has been publishing about system and database administration on his blog, www.LifeAfterCoffe.com since 2005. Jon often answers technical questions submitted to his blog by readers and also authored the popular Caffeine WordPress theme (www.lifeaftercoffee.com/caffeine/), a theme which is designed specifically to be easy to customize. Jon's blog continues to receive acclaim from the online community.

In addition to his technical abilities Jon has also been called upon to teach a college course in database management systems.

Originally from Maine, Jon now lives in Concord, NH and enjoys kayaking, skiing, hunting, flying radio controlled model airplanes, playing guitar, and cooking.